John F. Stoddard

The Intellectual Arithmetic

Designed for schools and academies; containing an extensive collection of practical

questions, with concise and original methods odf solution, which simplify many of

the most important rules of written arithmetic

.

John F. Stoddard

The Intellectual Arithmetic
*Designed for schools and academies; containing an extensive collection of practical
questions, with concise and original methods odf solution, which simplify many of the most
important rules of written arithmetic*

ISBN/EAN: 9783337373658

Printed in Europe, USA, Canada, Australia, Japan

Cover: Foto ©Thomas Meinert / pixelio.de

More available books at **www.hansebooks.com**

REVISED EDITION.

THE

Intellectual Arithmetic,

DESIGNED FOR

SCHOOLS AND ACADEMIES;

CONTAINING

AN EXTENSIVE COLLECTION OF PRACTICAL QUESTIONS,
WITH CONCISE AND ORIGINAL METHODS OF SOLU-
TION, WHICH SIMPLIFY MANY OF THE
MOST IMPORTANT RULES OF
WRITTEN ARITHMETIC.

By JOHN F. STODDARD, A.M.,

AUTHOR OF THE "NORMAL MATHEMATICAL SERIES," ETC.

Authorized by the Minister of Education for Ontario.

TORONTO:
CANADA PUBLISHING COMPANY
(LIMITED).

MDCCCLXXIX.

PREFACE.

NEITHER a desire of pecuniary gain nor a wish to appear as an author, prompted the presentation of this work to the public. Having felt the necessity of a more extended and systematic Intellectual Arithmetic for the younger, as well as more advanced pupils, I prepared and used in manuscript, in my own school, for a number of years, such a series of questions as I deemed best adapted to the purpose. After observing the superior mental training derived from their use, and the ease with which pupils thus trained comprehended the more advanced branches of mathematics, I venture to submit them to the public in the following pages, hoping that they may prove as useful to other schools as they have to my own.

The rule which I have observed in its preparation is to tell but one thing at a time, and that in its proper place.

It would be laborious to point out all the particulars in which this work differs from others of a similar character ; I shall, therefore, give only a brief exposition of its general plan, leaving the other differences (which, doubtless, will be considered of importance) to be found by those who study the book.

Chapters First, Second, Third, and *Fourth,* treat respectively of Addition, Subtraction, Multiplica-

tion and Division of simple numbers; each of
which is rendered familiar by an extensive collection of practical questions. The last Lesson in
Chapter Second consists of questions which combine
Addition and Subtraction ; the last Lesson in
Chapter Third, of questions combining Addition,
Subtraction, and Multiplication. Thus, an inti-
mate connection between Lessons and even
Chapters is kept up through the entire work, with
the exception of *Chapter Fifth*, which contains a
few of the most important tables of Weights and
Measures; each of which is illustrated with
appropriate questions.

Chapter Sixth is devoted to the subject of
Fractions, and contains twenty lessons, in which
many original combinations and concise solutions
occur.

Chapter Seventh consists of practical and intricate
questions of various kinds, which require for their
solution a thorough knowledge of the preceding
Chapters. This Chapter (which, it is believed, is
not contained in any similar work,) when thoroughly
understood, will be of incalculable benefit to those
who are studying, or intend to study Algebra.

Chapter Eighth includes Interest, Discount, and
per cent. of every description, in their various
modifications. The method of treating these sub-
jects is original, and renders the rules in Written
Arithmetics, under these heads (which are often
incomprehensible to pupils) perfectly intelligible,
by reducing the whole to one continued train of
reasoning.

It is believed that this Chapter, if thoroughly taught, can not fail to quicken, strengthen, and develope the reasoning powers; bringing into exercise, as it does, nearly every principle taught in the twenty lessons of *Chapter Sixth*, and also the greater part of *Chapter Seventh*, it must of necessity cause the pupil to acquire the habit of systematically classifying his knowledge, that he may, at any time, be able to call to his aid such portions of it as will assist him in illustrating or demonstrating the subject under consideration.

The mind is composed of a variety of faculties which require for their development appropriate and constant exercise. That Intellectual Arithmetic, when properly taught, is better calculated than any other study to invigorate and develope these faculties, to produce accurate and close discrimination, and to enable the pupil to acquire a knowledge of the Higher Mathematics with greater ease, can not for a moment admit of a doubt.

J. F. STODDARD.

New York, August ; 1860.

Suggestions to Teachers.

For the benefit of those whose experience is limited, I make the following suggestions in regard to the most approved methods of teaching this important branch of study:

The lesson should be assigned previous to recitation, to afford the pupils an opportunity for its examination; the use of the book, by the pupil, during class exercise, should be prohibited.

A question should be read slowly and distinctly, and the pupil required to repeat and analyze it without interruption, unless it be to make necessary criticism or correction.

The pupils should be called upon promiscuously, and not in rotation, to take part in the recitation.

Care should be taken that the language they use be strictly correct as to construction and articulation.

If not carefully guarded, pupils, in their hurried solutions, pronounce many simple words incorrectly. For instance, the words: *and, of, if, for, with, what, which, where, when, costs, quarts,* etc., are not unfrequently pronounced: *an, off, ef, fur, withe, wat, witch, ware, wen, coss, quats,* etc.

By careful attention to these particulars, a lesson in Intellectual Arithmetic is a practical lesson in elocution, grammar, rhetoric and logic, as well as a lesson in the science of numbers.

It is respectfully suggested that the particular forms given for the solution of questions be adhered to, unless *better* ones should be devised by the teacher.   J. F. S.

ARITHMETIC.

CHAPTER I.

Lesson I.

1.   2   and   1   are   how   many?

SOLUTION.—Two and one are 3.

2.   2   and   2   are   how   many?
3.   2   and   3   are   how   many?
4.   2   and   4   are   how   many?
5.   2   and   5   are   how   many?
6.   2   and   6   are   how   many?
7.   2   and   7   are   how   many?
8.   2   and   8   are   how   many?
9.   2   and   9   are   how   many?
10.   3   and   2   are   how   many?
11.   3   and   3   are   how   many?
12.   3   and   4   are   how   many?
13.   3   and   5   are   how   many?
14.   3   and   6   are   how   many?
15.   3   and   7   are   how   many?
16.   3   and   8   are   how   many?
17.   3   and   9   are   how   many?
18.   4   and   3   are   how   many?
19.   4   and   4   are   how   many?
20.   4   and   5   are   how   many?
21.   4   and   6   are   how   many?
22.   4   and   7   are   how   many?
23.   4   and   8   are   how   many?
24.   4   and   9   are   how   many?

25. James killed 2 birds and John 1; how many did both kill?

SOLUTION.—If James killed 2 birds and John 1, they together killed 2 birds and 1 bird, which are 3 birds.

26. I gave 2 cents to Henry and 2 cents to Harvey, how many cents did both receive?

27. Hiram had 2 cents, and his brother gave him 3 more; how many had he then?

28. George gave me 2 apples, and Mary gave me 4; how many did both give me?

29. A man had 2 cows, and he purchased 5 more; how many cows had he then?

30. John's father gave him 2 oranges, and his mother gave him 6; how many did he receive in all?

31. Philo bought 2 peaches, and his brother gave him 7; how many had he then?

32. Philip gave me 2 plums, and Myron gave me 8; how many did they together give me?

33. A farmer had 2 horses, and bought 9 more; how many had he then?

34. William had 3 oranges, and Moses gave him 2 more; how many had he then?

35. John bought 3 apples, and I gave him 3; how many had he then?

36. Philip gave 3 cents for some nuts, and 4 cents for some candy; how many cents did he pay for both?

37. I paid 3 cents for some wafers, and 5 cents for a stamp; how much did both cost me?

38. A merchant bought 3 barrels of sugar and 6 barrels of molasses; how many barrels did he buy?

39. Ralph is 3 years old, and Edward is 7; what is the sum of their ages?

40. A lemon cost 3 cents, and a pine-apple cost 8; how much did both cost?

41. James solved 3 questions in arithmetic, and Oliver 9; how many did both solve?

42. If it take 4 yards of cloth for a coat, and 3 for a vest, how many yards will it take for both?

43. Samuel bought 4 marbles, and found 4; how many had he then?

44. Isaac bought 4 sheets of paper, and I gave him 5; how many had he then?

45. A man bought a peck of apples for 4 cents, and a peck of pears for 6 cents; how much did the apples and pears together cost?

46. If Mary has 4 books, and her father should give her 7, how many books would she then have?

47. William has 4 marbles in his hand, and 8 in his pocket; how many has he in all?

48. Charles walked 4 miles, and rode 9; how far did he go?

49. In a certain class there are 5 boys, and 4 girls; how many pupils are there in the class?

Lesson II.

1.	5	and	4	are	how many?
2.	5	and	5	are	how many?
3.	5	and	6	are	how many?
4.	5	and	7	are	how many?
5.	5	and	8	are	how many?
6.	5	and	9	are	how many?
7.	6	and	5	are	how many?
8.	6	and	6	are	how many?
9.	6	and	7	are	how many?
10.	6	and	8	are	how many?
11.	6	and	9	are	how many?
12.	7	and	6	are	how many?
13.	7	and	7	are	how many?
14.	7	and	8	are	how many?
15.	7	and	9	are	how many?

16.	8	and	7	are now	many?
17.	8	and	8	are how	many?
18.	8	and	9	are how	many?
19.	8	and	5	are how	many?
20.	9	and	6	are how	many?
21.	9	and	8	are how	many?
22.	9	and	9	are how	many?
23.	9	and	10	are how	many?
24.	9	and	7	are how	many?
25.	9	and	11	are how	many?

26. Mary has answered 5 questions correctly and 4 incorrectly; how many questions was she asked?

27. A beggar met two boys; one gave him 5 cents, and the other gave him 6 cents; how many cents did they together give him?

28. A man bought a hat for 5 dollars, and a pair of boots for 6 dollars; how much was the cost of both?

29. There are 9 boys on one bench and 8 on another; how many are there on both?

30. Maria gave her teacher 5 pinks and 7 roses; how many flowers did she give him?

31. Harry caught 5 squirrels, and Henry caught 8; how many did both catch?

32. If we learn 5 pages this week, and 9 next, how many shall we learn in two weeks?

33. Frank sold a melon for 6 cents, and an orange for 5 cents; how many cents did he receive for both?

34. John bought 6 whips, and Joseph gave him 6; how many had he then?

35. George had 6 chestnuts, and Richard gave him 7; how many had he then?

36. Henry bought 6 candies, and Sarah bought 8; how many were bought by both?

37. Rebecca has 6 oranges, and Catharine has 9; how many oranges have both?

38. A boy bought 7 apples, and his father gave him 6; how many had he then?

39. Minerva bought 7 yards of ribbon, and her mother gave her 6; how many yards did she then have?

40. There were 7 boys sitting on one bench, and 8 on another; how many were on both?

41. There were 7 boys at play, and 9 other boys joined them; how many were there in all?

42. If I have 8 cents in one hand, and 7 in the other, how many have I in both?

43. If Mary has 8 peaches, and Margaret has 9, how many have both?

44. Sally gave 9 cents for some thread, and 7 cents for some needles; how much did the needles and thread cost her?

45. Charles has 9 marbles, and Albert has 5; how many marbles have Charles and Albert?

46. 9 birds were in a tree, and 6 were on the ground; how many were there in all?

47. Sarah gave 9 cents for some cinnamon, and 7 cents for some raisins; how many cents did these cost her?

48. George shot 9 pigeons, and James shot 8; how many did both shoot?

49. Russel caught 7 fish, and Robert caught 5; how many did both catch?

50. In one field there are 8 horses, and in another there are 9; how many are there in both?

Lesson III.

1. How many are 10 and 2? 10 and 3? 10 and 4? 10 and 5? 10 and 6? 10 and 7? 10 and 9? 10 and 8? 10 and 10?

2. How many are 2 and 2? 2 and 12? 2 and 22? 2 and 32? 2 and 42? 2 and 52? 2 and 62? 2 and 7?? 2 and 82? 2 and 92?

3. How many are 3 and 3?   3 and 13?   3 and 23 ?
3 and 33? 3 and 43? 3 and 53? 3 and 63? 3 and 73?
3 and 83? 3 and 93? 96 and 4?

4. How many are 4 and 4?   4 and 14?   4 and 24?
4 and 34? 4 and 44?   4 and 54? 4 and 64?   4 and
74? 4 and 84? 4 and 94? 98 and 2?

5. How many are 5 and 5?   5 and 15? 5 and 25?
5 and 35? 5 and 45? 5 and 55? 5 and 65? 5 and 75?
5 and 85? 5 and 95?

6. How many are 6 and 6? 6 and 16? 6 and 26?
6 and 36? 6 and 46? 6 and 56? 6 and 66 ? 6 and 76?
6 and 96?

7. How many are 7 and 7?   7 and 17?   7 and 27 ?
7 and 37?   7 and 47?   7 and 57?   7 and 67?   7 and
77? 7 and 87? 7 and 97?

8. How many are 8 and 8?   8 and 18?   8 and 28?
8 and 38? 8 and 48? 8 and 58? 8 and 68? 8 and 78?
8 and 88? 8 and 98 ?

9. How many are 9 and 9?   9 and 19?   9 and 29?
9 and 39? 9 and 49? 9 and 59 ? 9 and 69? 9 and 79 ?
9 and 89? 9 and 99?

10. How many are 10 and 11? 10 and 21? 10 and
31? 10 and 41? 10 and 51?   10 and 61?   10 and 71?
10 and 81? 10 and 91 ?

11. How many are 10 and 12? 10 and 22? 10 and
32? 10 and 42? 10 and 52? 10 and 62? 10 and 72?
10 and 82? 10 and 92 ?

12. How many are 10 and 4? 10 and 14? 10 and
24? 10 and 34? 10 and 44? 10 and 54? 10 and 64?
10 and 74? 10 and 84? 10 and 94?

13. How many are 11 and 3? 11 and 13? 11 and
23? 11 and 33? 11 and 43 ? 11 and 53? 11 and 63?
11 and 73? 11 and 83? 11 and 93?

14. How many are 11 and 4? 11 and 14? 11 and
24? 11 and 34? 11 and 44? 11 and 54? 11 and 64?
11 and 74? 11 and 84? 11 and 94?

15. How many are 10 and 5? 10 and 15? 10 and

35? 10 and 45? 10 and 55? 10 and 65? 10 and 75?
10 and 85? 10 and 95? 10 and 25?

16. How many are 11 and 5? 11 and 15? 11 and
25? 11 and 35? 11 and 45? 11 and 55? 11 and 65?
11 and 75? 11 and 85? 11 and 95?

17. How many are 3 and 8? 3 and 18? 3 and 28?
3 and 38? 3 and 48? 3 and 58? 3 and 68? 3 and 78?
3 and 88? 3 and 98?

18. How many are 8 and 4? 8 and 14? 8 and 24?
8 and 34? 8 and 44? 8 and 54? 8 and 64? 8 and 74?
8 and 84? 8 and 94?

19. How many are 7 and 7? 7 and 17? 7 and 27?
7 and 37? 7 and 47? 7 and 57? 7 and 67? 7 and 77?
7 and 87? 7 and 97?

20. How many are 8 and 6? 8 and 16? 8 and 26?
8 and 36? 8 and 46? 8 and 56? 8 and 66? 8 and 76?
8 and 86? 8 and 96?

Lesson IV.

1.	8	and	9	are	now	many?
2.	11	and	7	are	how	many?
3.	10	and	9	are	how	many?
4.	7	and	14	are	how	many?
5.	6	and	12	are	how	many?
6.	9	and	15	are	how	many?
7.	11	and	18	are	how	many?
8.	15	and	12	are	how	many?
9.	14	and	13	are	how	many?
10.	16	and	14	are	how	many?
11.	21	and	12	are	how	many?
12.	24	and	13	are	how	many?
13.	25	and	15	are	how	many?
14.	27	and	13	are	how	many?
15.	23	and	17	are	how	many?

16.	29	and	11	are	how	many ?
17.	30	and	20	are	how	many ?
18.	34	and	15	are	how	many ?
19.	32	and	18	are	how	many ?

REMARK.—The Symbol $=$ is the sign of *equality*, and when placed between two quantities it denotes that they are equal to each other. Thus 10 cents $=$ 1 dime, is read, 10 cents *equal* 1 dime.

The Symbol $+$ is called *plus*, and denotes that the quantities between which it is placed, are to be added. Thus, $4+2=6$, shows that 4 and 2 are to be added: and is read, *four plus two equals* 6.

20. $33+44$ are how many?
21. $35+15$ are how many?
22. $36+12$ are how many?
23. $40+36$ are how many?
24. $40+29$ are how many?
25. $44+20$ are how many?
26. $48+32$ are how many?
27. $45+35$ are how many?
28. $4+8+6$ are how many?
29. $8+2+7$ are how many?
30. $10+7+3$ are how many?
31. $12+10+9$ are how many?
32. $15+12+6$ are how many?
33. $18+4+10$ are how many?
34. $24+16+12$ are how many?
35. $22+33+11$ are how many?
36. $15+16+2$ are how many?
37. $28+12+15$ are how many?
38. $46+24+19$ are how many?
39. $12+8+6+4$ are how many?
40. $24+10+6+12$ are how many?
41. $22+32+6-10$ are how many?
42. $37+23+15$ are how many?
43. $64+26+12-8$ are how many?

Lesson V.

1. Three boys, James, Joseph, and Jacob, gave some money to a beggar; James gave him 6, Joseph 8, and Jacob 10 cents; how many cents did they give him?

2. Give 8 cents to John, 4 cents to Morgan, and 2 cents to Samuel; how many cents did all receive?

3. Henry has 3 marbles, Harvey has 10, and Harry has 7; how many marbles have all?

4. Give 7 nuts to one boy, 6 to another, and 7 to another; how many nuts did the three boys receive?

5. Bought a basket of strawberries for 7 cents, a basket of cherries for 4 cents, and a basket of plums for 8 cents; how many cents did all cost?

6. Lydia has 9 pinks, Mary 10, and Ann 7; how many pinks have they all?

7. Bought a knife for 14 cents, and a ball for 12 cents; how much did both cost?

8. Gave 18 cents for an arithmetic, 2 for a pencil, and 10 for a slate; how much did all cost?

9. James had 12 cents, and his mother gave him 13 more; how many had he then?

10. Robert shot 9 birds, Richard shot 11, and James shot 12; how many did they shoot?

11. A boy bought a pound of butter for 14 cents, a pound of meat for 8 cents, and a bunch of lettuce for 7 cents; how many cents did these articles cost?

12. Bought a pound of raisins for 10 cents, a pound of candies for 12 cents, and a pound of cinnamon for 15 cents; how much was the whole cost?

13. John had 20 marbles, Matthew 9, and Morgan 12; how many had they in all?

14. James bought a pigeon for 9 cents, a robin for 10 cents, and a squirrel for 12 cents; how much did all cost him?

15. A lady bought some pins for 15 cents, some

thread for 10 cents, and some lace for 18 cents; how many cents did all these articles cost her?

16. A gentleman bought a hat for 6 dollars, a vest for 5 dollars, and a coat for 20 dollars; how many dollars did he pay for them all?

17. A man bought a watch for 40 dollars, a gold chain for 15 dollars, and a gold pen for 5 dollars; how much did he pay for these three articles?

18. Jackson gave 25 cents to his sister, and 23 to his mother; how many cents did he give away?

19. Bought a barrel of flour for 7 dollars, a barrel of pork for 12 dollars, and a barrel of fish for 11 dollars; how much was the whole cost?

20. Bought a horse for 60 dollars, a cow for 20 dollars, and a colt for 25 dollars; how much did all cost?

21. If your father should give you 12 cents, your mother 14 cents, and your sister 4 cents, how many cents would you then have?

22. A boy spent 12 cents for confectionery, 9 cents for a ball, and 5 cents for a top; how many cents did he spend for all?

23. A man bought some butter for 57 dollars, and some molasses for 23 dollars; how many dollars did both cost?

24. A boy travelled 17 miles one day, and 23 the next; how far did he travel in the two days?

25. A lady bought a hat for 7 dollars, a dress for 9 dollars, and a gold watch for 60 dollars; how many dollars did all cost?

26. A mechanic sold a wagon for 57 dollars, and a sleigh for 43 dollars; how much did he receive for both?

27. A boy saw 24 pigeons on one tree, and 36 on another; how many did he see in all?

28. In a certain recitation 21 questions were answered correctly, and 9 incorrectly; how many questions were asked during the recitation?

29. Gave 87 dollars for a chaise, 2 dollars for a whip, and 11 dollars for a buffalo robe; how much was given for all?

30. If a horse is worth 60 dollars, and a chaise 75 dollars, what is the value of both?

31. Matthew is 15 years old, Morgan is 7, and Martin is 10; what is the sum of their ages?

32. A man bought a load of hay for 7 dollars, a load of rye for 36 dollars, and a load of wheat for 57 dollars; how much was the whole cost?

33. A man is 48 years old, and his wife is 32 years old; what is the sum of their ages?

34. A farmer bought a horse for 60 dollars, and a yoke of oxen for 75 dollars; how much did the horse and oxen together cost him?

35. John gave 11 candies to his brother, 9 to his sister, and kept 12 himself; how many candies had he at first?

36. Simeon hoed 12 rows of corn, Simon 15, James 13, and John 11; how many rows did they together hoe?

37. A merchant sold 30 barrels of flour one week, 37 the next week, and 33 the following week; how many barrels did he sell during the three weeks?

38. A merchant sold a barrel of sugar for 25 dollars, a barrel of rum for 15 dollars, and a hogshead of molasses for 23 dollars; how much did he receive for all these articles?

39. A man bought a firkin of butter for 9 dollars, a keg of molasses for 7 dollars, a box of cheese for 4 dollars, and a box of raisins for 5 dollars; how much was the entire cost?

40. A lady bought a silk dress for 18 dollars, a muff for 11 dollars, a shawl for 17 dollars, and a pair of gloves for 1 dollar; the entire cost is required.

2

CHAPTER II.

Lesson I.

1. If I have 3 apples, and give 1 of them to Richard how many shall I have left?

SOLUTION.—If I have 3 apples and give 1 to Richard, I shall have remaining the difference between 3 and 1, which is 2 apples.

2. William had 4 chestnuts, and gave 1 to his brother; how many had he left?

3. Martha had 5 books, and on her way to school lost one of them; how many had she left?

4. Cornelia had 6 apples, and gave 1 to her brother; how many had she left?

5. Rachel had 10 pins, and lost 1 of them; how many had she left?

6. Martha had 12 pears, and gave 2 to Elizabeth; how many had she left?

7. If you had 5 candies, and should give 2 of them away, how many would you have left?

8. James had 6 apples, and gave 2 away; how many had he remaining?

9. Cornelia says she learned 12 letters yesterday, and has forgotten 3 of them; how many does she remember?

10. James had 10 marbles, and lost 3; how many had he left?

11. Mary found 9 roses on her bush, and picked off 4 of them; how many remained on the bush?

12. How many are 4 less 2?
13. How many are 5 less 3?
14. How many are 6 less 3?
15. How many are 9 less 4?
16. How many are 9 less 3?

17. How many are 9 less 7?
18. How many are 6 less 5?
19. How many are 11 less 4?
20. How many are 10 less 4?
21. How many are 11 less 5?
22. How many are 14 less 4?
23. How many are 8 less 5?
24. How many are 13 less 3?
25. How many are 14 less 5?
26. How many are 17 less 7?
27. How many are 15 less 5?
28. How many are 13 less 10?
29. How many are 23 less 3?
30. How many are 27 less 7?

REMARK—The symbol —, is called *minus*, and denotes that the quantity on the right of it is to be taken from the quantity on the left. Thus, $6-4=2$, shows that 4 is to be subtracted from 6; and is read, 6 *minus* 4 *equal* 2.

31. $8-5$ are how many?
32. $9-7$ are how many?
33. $10-8$ are how many?
34. $11-8$ are how many?
35. $12-6$ are how many?
36. $13-8$ are how many?
37. $14-8$ are how many?
38. $18-8$ are how many?
39. $22-12$ are how many?
40. $24-14$ are how many?
41. $12-4$ are how many?
42. $28-8$ are how many?
43. $20-5$ are how many?
44. $20-8$ are how many?
45. $20-9$ are how many?
46. $20-7$ are how many?
47. $20-10$ are how many?
48. $20-15$ are how many?
49. $24-10$ are how many?

50.	25—10+5	are	how	many?
51.	26—10+4	are	how	many?
52.	28—10+5	are	how	many?
53.	27—10+5	are	how	many?
54.	29—10+6	are	how	many?
55.	32—10+8	are	how	many?
56.	34—10+7	are	how	many?
57.	36—10+8	are	how	many?
58.	35—10+4	are	how	many?
59.	37—10+7	are	how	many?
60.	38—10+8	are	how	many?
61.	39—10+9	are	how	many?
62.	47—10+6	are	how	many?
63.	40—12+9	are	how	many?
64.	42—20+7	are	how	many!
65.	45—20+5	are	how	many!
66.	45—20+6	are	how	many!
67.	47—20+8	are	how	many!
68.	47—37+4	are	how	many!
69.	49—19+9	are	how	many?
70.	52—22+10	are	how	many!
71.	54—34+11	are	how	many!
72.	26—46+22	are	how	many!
73.	57—27+14	are	how	many?
74.	58—48+9	are	how	many?.
75.	62—30+10	are	how	many?
76.	55—40+15	are	how	many?
77.	68—48+16	are	how	many?
78.	74—34+15	are	how	many?

79. Gave 7 cents for a spool of thread, and 4 cents for a lemon; how much more did the thread cost than the lemon?

80. Paid 18 cents for a pound of butter, and 8 cents for a pound of meat; how much more was paid for the butter than for the meat?

81. James bought 18 candies, and gave John 7 of them; how many had he left?

82. Sold a quantity of wool for 27 dollars, and received in payment a barrel of flour worth 5 dollars ; how many dollars remain due?

83. James has 27 marbles, and John has 17; how many more has James than John?

84. Harry is 15 years old, and Henry is 9 years old; how many years older is Harry than Henry?

85. A teacher being asked how many pupils he had, answered that he usually had 37, but at present he had only 27; how many were absent?

86. A man purchased a watch for 37 dollars, but found he had only 24 dollars with him; how much must he borrow to pay the balance?

87. A has 94 sheep, and B has 44; how many more sheep has A than B?

88. Morgan gave 23 cents for some cake, and 14 cents for some cinnamon; how much more did the cake cost than the cinnamon?

89. Michael had 29 cents, and lost 14; how many had he left?

90. In a certain recitation 47 questions were asked, and 9 of them were answered incorrectly; how many were answered correctly?

91. A man sold 23 sheep from a flock consisting of 93; how many sheep remained?

92. Mr. B. bought a horse for 35 dollars, and sold it for 46 dollars; how much did he gain?

93. A cow was bought for 25 dollars and sold for 19 dollars; how much was the loss?

94. A merchant bought a quantity of goods for 95 dollars, but being damaged was obliged to sell them for 80 dollars; how much did he lose?

95. From a vessel containing 57 gallons, 27 gallons leaked out; how much remained in it ?

96. A merchant bought a quantity of silk for 47 dollars, and sold it for 67 dollars; how much did he gain by the bargain?

97. A butcher has 57 sheep, and 44 lambs; how many more sheep has he than lambs?

98. Paid 97 dollars for a quantity of sugar, and 43 dollars for some molasses; how much more did the sugar cost than the molasses?

Lesson II.

CHAPTER FIRST COMBINED WITH THE PRECEDING LESSON.

1. A boy has 7 chestnuts in one hand, and 4 in the other; how many more has he in one hand than in the other ; and how many in both?

2. Bought a barrel of fish for 8 dollars, and some quinces for 3 dollars; how much more did the fish cost than the quinces ? What was the cost of both?

3. Gave 15 dollars for a cow and 6 dollars for a sheep; how much more was given for the cow than for the sheep? How much was given for both?

4. Phineas gave 50 cents for a grammar, and 25 cents for an arithmetic; how much was the cost of both ? How much did one cost more than the other?

5. Paid 15 dollars for a barrel of rum, and 6 dollars for a barrel of flour; how much was the cost of both; and how much more did the rum cost than the flour?

6. Sold a firkin of butter for 10 dollars, a keg of cheese for 5 dollars, and received in payment a barrel of flour worth 6 dollars ; how much remains due?

7. James gave 12 cents for oranges, 15 cents for cake, and had 13 cents remaining; how much had he at first?

8. Mary bought a comb for 10 cents, a spool of thread for 12 cents, and a paper of needles for 8 cents ; she handed the clerk 37 cents; how much change ought she to receive?

9. A man sold a cow for 20 dollars, a calf for 4 dollars, and a sheep for 3 dollars, and in payment received a waggon worth 17 dollars ; how much remains due ?

10. A lady bought a ribbon for 24 cents, some tape for 8 cents, and some thread for 12 cents, she had only 60 cents ; how much remained after she paid for these articles?

11. Stephen, at a game of marbles, won 4 and lost 6, and then had only 8 remaining; how many had he at first?

12 Sampson having 9 apples, gave 4 to his mother, and 3 to his sister; for his generosity his fat.er gave him 13 more ; how many had he then ?

13. A man bought some cloth for 12 dollars and sold it for 18 dollars ; how much was his gain ?

14. A farmer bought a horse for 63 dollars, and exchanged it for a yoke of oxen,—these he sold for 87 dollars; how much did he gain by the operation?

15. A man bought a yoke of oxen for 97 dollars, their services amounted to 40 dollars, and their keeping to 13 dollars,—he then sold them for 80 dollars ; did he gain or lose, and how much ?

16. A box of raisins was bought for 3 dollars, a firkin of butter for 15 dollars, and were both sold for 20 dollars; how much was gained?

17. A farmer sold a cow for 29 dollars, which was 5 dollars more than she cost ; how much did she cost?

18. A drover bought some sheep for 40 dollars, some cattle for 130 dollars, and sold them all for 200 dollars ; how much was his gain?

19. A jeweller bought a watch for 20 dollars, a chain for 40 dollars, a key for 2 dollars, and sold them all for 42 dollars; how much did he gain by the bargain?

20. 24+12+9 are how many ?

21. 10+30+15 are how many ?

22. 14+16+11 are how many?
23. 36+9—12 are how many?
24. 38+22—15 are how many?
25. 43+37—20 are how many?
26. 13+26—25 are how many?
27. 44—22+10—12 are how many?
28. 27+23—20+2 are how many?
29. 15+25—30+15 are how many?
30. 20+40—30+10 are how many?

31. A boy bought a ball for 6 cents; for how much must he sell it to gain 4?

32. A merchant bought a hogshead of molasses for 47 dollars, and paid 3 dollars for cartage; for how much must he sell it to gain 12 dollars?

33. A grocer bought a hogshead of sugar for 30 dollars; for what must he sell it to gain 18 dollars?

34. A drover bought sheep as follows; of one man he bought 24, of another 8, and of another 22,—he then sold 20 of them; how many remained unsold?

35. A watch cost 40 dollars; how must it be sold to gain 13 dollars?

36. Four boys bought a melon; one gave 3 cents, another 4, another 8, and the other 6; how much did they pay for the melon?

37. Mary bought 16 candies at one shop, and 13 at another,—on her way home she ate 11 of them; how many had she left?

38. Matthew had 9 nuts, Mary gave him 10 more, and John gave him enough to make his number 39; how many did John give him?

39. A farmer had 25 sheep in one field and 15 in another,—he then bought enough more to make his number 56; how many did he buy?

40. John has 34 marbles, and Albert 25; how many have they both; and how many more has John than Albert?

CHAPTER III.

Lesson I.

1. Two times 1 are how many?
2. Two times 2 are how many?
3. Two times 3 are how many?
4. Two times 4 are how many?
5. Two times 5 are how many?
6. Two times 6 are how many?
7. Two times 7 are how many?
8. Two times 8 are how many?
9. Two times 9 are how many?
10. Two times 10 are how many?
11. Two times 11 are how many?
12. Two times 12 are how many?
13. What will 2 oranges cost at 3 cents apiece?

SOLUTION.—If one orange cost 3 cents, 2 oranges will cost two times 3 cents ; which are 6 cents.

14. What will 2 peaches cost, at 2 cents apiece?
15. What will 2 apples cost, at 3 cents apiece?
16. What will 2 pine-apples cost, at 8 cents apiece?
17. What will 2 pounds of meat cost, at 5 cents a pound?
18. What will 2 pounds of cinnamon cost, at 11 cents a pound?
19. What will 2 pounds of raisins cost, at 12 cents a pound?
20. What will 2 citrons cost, at 10 cents apiece?
21. What will 2 quarts of cherries cost, at 9 cents a quart?
22. What will 2 lemons cost, at 4 cents apiece?
23. Three times 2 are how many?
24. Three times 3 are how many?
25. Three times 4 are how many?

26. Three times 5 are how many?
27. Three times 6 are how many?
28. Three times 7 are how many?
29. Three times 8 are how many?
30. Three times 9 are how many?
31. Three times 10 are how many?
32. Three times 11 are how many?
33. Three times 12 are how many?
34. Four times 3 are how many?
35. Four times 4 are how many?
36. Four times 5 are how many?
37. Four times 6 are how many?
38. Four times 7 are how many?
39. Four times 8 are how many?
40. Four times 9 are how many?
41. Four times 10 are how many?
42. Four times 11 are how many?
43. Four times 12 are how many?

44. What will 3 quarts of cherries cost, at 6 cents a quart?

45. What will 3 lead pencils cost, at 5 cents apiece?

46. What will 3 quarts of milk cost, at 4 cents a quart?

47. What will 3 yards of ribbon cost, at 7 cents a yd?

48. What will 4 quarts of chestnuts cost, at 6 cents a quart?

49. What will 4 yards of edging cost, at 5 cents a yd?

50. What will 3 ounces of snuff cost, at 8 cents an ounce?

51. What will 4 ounces of cinnamon cost, at 7 cents an ounce?

52. What will 3 pounds of cheese cost, at 10 cents a pound?

53. What will 4 sheets of wadding cost, at 8 cents a sheet?

54. What will 3 yards of calico cost at 11 cents a yd!

55. What will 4 skeins of silk cost, at 9 cts. a skein?

56. What will 3 yards of ribbon cost, at 12 cents a yard?

57. What will 4 pounds of starch cost, at 12 cents a pound?

58. What will 4 candlesticks cost, at 11 cents apiece?

59. What will 4 tops cost, at 10 cents apiece?

60. What will 5 apples cost, at 4 cents apiece?

61. Five times 6 are how many?
62. Five times 7 are how many?
63. Five times 8 are how many?
64. Five times 5 are how many?
65. Five times 10 are how many?
66. Five times 9 are how many?
67. Five times 12 are how many?
68. Five times 11 are how many?
69. Six times 6 are how many?
70. Six times 8 are how many?
71. Six times 7 are how many?
72. Six times 10 are how many?
73. Six times 9 are how many?
74. Six times 12 are how many?
75. Six times 11 are how many?
76. Seven times 6 are how many?
77. Seven times 8 are how many?
78. Seven times 7 are how many?
79. Seven times 10 are how many?
80. Seven times 9 are how many?
81. Seven times 12 are how many?
82. Seven times 11 are how many?

83. What will 5 barrels of flour cost, at 6 dollars a barrel?

84. What will 5 bushels of potatoes cost, at 5 dimes a bushel?

85. What will 6 primers cost, at 6 cents apiece?

86. What will 5 barrels of fish cost, at 7 dollars a barrel?

87. What will 6 pounds of mutton cost, at 7 cents a pound?

88. What will 5 barrels of sugar cost, at 12 dollars a barrel?

89. What will 6 pounds of sturgeon cost, at 10 cents a pound?

90. What will 6 pounds of almonds cost, at 12 cents a pound?

91. What will 5 barrels of pork cost, at $10 a bbl.?

92. What will 6 pounds of candles cost, at 9c. a lb.?

93. What will five coats cost, at 9 dollars apiece?

94. What will 6 handkerchiefs cost, at 11 cents apiece.

95. What will 6 inkstands cost, at 8 cents apiece?

96. What will 7 lamps cost, at 9 dimes apiece?

97. What will 7 plows cost, at 8 dollars apiece?

98. What will 7 boxes of caps cost, at 10c. a box?

99. What will 7 quires of paper cost, at 11 cents a quire?

100 What will 7 letter-folders cost, at 11 cents apiece?

101. Eight times 8 are how many?
102. Eight times 10 are how many?
103. Nine times 8 are how many?
104. Eight times 7 are how many?
105. Nine times 9 are how many?
106. Eight times 9 are how many?
107. Nine times 11 are how many?
108. Eight times 12 are how many?
109. Nine times 10 are how many?
110. Eight times 11 are how many?
111. Nine times 12 are how many?

112. What will 9 bunches of roses cost, at 9 cents a bunch.

113. What will 8 pen-knives cost, at 12 cts. apiece?

114. What will 9 bunches of grapes cost, at 12 cents a bunch.

115. What will 11 yards of calico cost, at 11 cents a yard?

116. What will 19 balls of cotton cost, at 12 cents a ball?

117. What will 11 pounds of ginger cost, at 12 cents a pound?

118. What will 10 blocks of tape cost, at 8 cents a block?

119. What will 12 yards of cloth cost, at 12 dimes a yard?

120. What will 13 pair of boots coot, at $4 a pair?

Lesson II.

CHAPTERS FIRST AND SECOND COMBINED WITH THE PRECEDING LESSON.

1. At 7 cents apiece, what will 9 pine-apples cost?

2. If the postage on 1 letter is 3 cents, what will be the postage on 8 letters?

3. If it require 8 yards of calico to make 1 dress, how many yards will it require to make 7 dresses?

4. If John obtain 2 credit marks in 1 day, how many will he have in 15 days?

5. A man hired a horse to ride 12 miles, at the rate of 5 cents a mile; how much must he pay?

6. Margaret's cloak contains 7 yards of merino, worth 9 dimes a yard; what is the value of her cloak?

7 If a stage-coach go 9 miles in an hour, how far will it go in 7 hours?

8. At 2 dollars a week, how much will 20 weeks' board come to?

9. The fare by railroad from Albany to Boston is 5 dollars for 1 person; how much will it be for a family of 9 persons?

10. Helen had 8 rose bushes, and there were 7 roses on each; how many roses had she in all?

11 At 3 dimes a gallon, what will 15 gallons of molasses cost?

12. There are 10 rows of trees in an orchard, and 12 trees in each row; how many trees are there in the orchard?

13. A traveller meeting 13 beggars, gave to each of them 3 dimes; how many dimes did he give to all of them?

14. A woman bought 11 yards of cloth and paid for it with butter,—giving 9 pounds for a yard; how many pounds of butter did it take to pay for the cloth? How much did the cloth cost, provided the butter was worth 10 cents a pound?

15. In a certain corn field there are 24 rows, and 30 hills in each row; how many hills in the field?

16. What will 40 steel pens cost, at 2 cents apiece?

17. What will 8 pair of snuffers cost, at 3 dimes a pair?

18. When 2 dimes are paid for 1 duck, what will be the cost of 8 ducks? of 10 ducks? of 12 ducks?

19. When hay is worth 8 dollars a ton, what is the value of 2 tons? of 4 tons? of 3 tons? of 7 tons? of 5 tons? of 10 tons? of 12 tons? of 14 tons?

20. At 2 dimes apiece, how many cents will 4 books cost? 6 books? 10 books? 12 books? 11 books? 7 books? 16 books? 13 books? 14 books?

21. If 5 cents will buy 1 primer, what will be the cost of 4 primers? of 6? of 9? of 8? of 10?

22. 6 plates, at 5 dimes apiece, will cost how much?

23. At a dime apiece, how much will 4 handkerchiefs cost? 6? 8? 10? 12? 11? 14? 16?

24. At 6 dimes apiece, how many cents will 2 geese cost? 4? 5? 8? 10? 12? 9? 7?

25. At 12 cents apiece, how much will 3 candle-sticks cost? How much will 6? 5? 8? 9? 10? 7?

26. If I pay 5 cents for riding 1 mile, how much must I pay for riding 7 miles? 8 miles? 6? 9? 10? 12?

27. At 7 cents a yard, how much will 5 yards of ribbon cost? 6 yards? 8 yards? 9 yards? 10 yards? 12 yards?

28. If a tooth-brush cost 18 cents, how much will 4 cost?

29. 9 turkeys will cost how much, at 8 dimes apiece?

30. At 14 cents a quire, how much will 2 quires of paper cost? 3 quires? 4 quires? 5 quires?

31. How much will 7 pictures cost, at 5 cents apiece? at 6 cents apiece? at 8 cents apiece? at 10 cents apiece?

32. How much will 8 knives cost, at 6 dimes apiece? at 10 dimes apiece?

33. At 10 dimes apiece, how much will 4 caps cost? 5? 6? 8? 9? 12? 14? 17? 19? 21? 25?

34. At 40 cents a day, how much will 2 days' work amount to? 5 days work?

35. If one paper of candy cost 6 cents, how much will 3 papers cost? 5 papers? 8 papers? 12 papers?

36. At 7 dollars a hundred, how much will 4 hundred feet of cedar boards cost? 9 hundred feet? 10 hundred feet?

37. If 1 bushel of wheat cost 60 cents, how much will 6 bushels cost? 4 bushels? 5 bushels?

38. How much will 8 muffs cost at 5 dollars each?

39. How much will 19 lead pencils cost, at 5 cents each?

40. How much will 11 boxes of cheese cost, at 4 dollar a box? at 5 dollars? at 8 dollars a box?

41. How much will 12 barrels of pork cost at 5 dollars a barrel? at 8 dollars? at 9 dollars? at 10 dollars?

42. How much will 9 tons of hay cost, at 13 dollar a ton?

43. James is 9 years old, and his father is 4 times as old as he is; how old is his father?

44. Jane's frock contains 7 yards of silk, worth 8 dimes a yard; what was the value of the silk? Provided the making cost 2 dollars, how much was the cost of her dress?

45. If a barrel of flour will serve 12 men 8 days, how long will it serve 1 man?

46. If I earn 12 dollars in a month, and spend 8, how much shall I have at the end of 12 months?

47. If I earn 12 dollars a month, and pay 25 cents a week for washing, and 2 dollars a week for board, how much will I have at the end of 40 weeks (10 months)?

48. If I buy 9 tons of hay, at 12 dollars a ton, and sell 6 tons, at 15 dollars a ton, and the 3 remaining tons at 10 dollars a ton, how much shall I gain by the operation?

49. Bought 11 yards of broadcloth, at 4 dollars a yard, but, being damaged, I was obliged to lose 18 dollars by the sale of it; how much did I receive for it?

50. If I buy 12 barrels of pork, at 8 dollars a barrel, and sell it all for 108 dollars, how much shall I gain by so doing?

51. A man bought a horse for 80 dollars, paid 2 dollars a week for his keeping, and received 4 dollars a week for his work;—at the expiration of 10 weeks he sold him for 70 dollars; how much did he gain by the operation?

52. For how much must I sell 4 barrels of wheat, which cost me 8 dollars a barrel, to gain 8 dollars?

53. What is the cost of 9 cows, at 25 dollars each?

54. Provided a hunter should kill 5 pigeons and wound 4 at every shot; how many would he kill and wound respectively, by shooting 8 times?

55. If a man travel 29 miles in a day, how many miles will he travel in 6 days?

56. How much will 8 months' wages amount to, at 18 dollars a month?

57. If 10 men eat 18 pounds of butter in 1 week, how long would it last 1 man?

58. If 80 dollars will pay for 4 dinners for 20 men, how many dinners would it buy for 1 man?

59. Bought 3 yards of cloth for a coat, at 7 dollars a yard, the buttons and cord cost 2 dollars, buckram and wadding 1 dollar,—paid for making it 6 dollars; for how much must I sell it to gain 5 dollars?

60. If 17 men can do a piece of work in 9 days, how many days would it take 1 man to perform the same work?

61. Two men start from the same place, and travel in opposite directions;—one at the rate of 7 miles an hour, the other, 9 miles an hour; how far apart will they be in 2 hours?

62. Two men start from the same place, and travel the same way;—one at the rate of 3 miles an hour, the other, 8 miles an hour; how far apart will they be at the end of 8 hours?

. 63. Two men are 50 miles apart, and approach each other;—one at the rate of 2 miles an hour, the other, 3 miles an hour; how far apart will they be at the end of 5 hours?

64. If 1 orange is worth 4 apples, how many apples must be given for 13 oranges?

65. A man earned 80 cents a day, and paid 50 cents a day for his board and washing; how much had he left at the expiration of 6 days?

66. Jane bought 4 yards of silk, at 2 dollars a yard, 3 shawls, at 10 dollars each, and some delaine for 10 dollars; she paid 5 ten-dollar bills; how much ought she to receive back?

67. Mary bought 5 yards of silk, at 8 dimes a yard,

3

and 8 yards of linen, at 9 dimes a yard; how many yards did she buy, and how much did all cost?

68. In a certain school there are 12 girls, and 3 times as many boys, less 8; how many boys in the school, and how many boys and girls together?

69. John has 7 books, and Mary has 4 times as many, less 18; how many has Mary, and how many have both?

70. Albert has 9 marbles, Aaron 3 times as many, less 7, and Amos has twice as many as both, less 8; how n any has each, and how many have they together?

71. Perry worked for Elisha 4 days, at 6 dimes a day;—Elisha gave him 7 bushels of corn, at 3 dimes a bushel; how much was then due Perry?

72. A merchant bought 25 pounds of sugar for 125 cents, and sold 15 pounds of it, at 6 cents a pound, and the remaining 10 pounds, at 4 cents a pound; how muce did he gain by so doing?

73. If the interest on 1 dollar for a year is 6 cents, how much is the interest on 13 dollars for the same time?

74. What will 27 pounds of beef cost, at 4 cents a pound?

75. When beef is 5 cents a pound, and pork 9 cents, how much more will 9 pounds of pork cost than 9 pounds of beef?

76. Mary bought 35 quarts of milk, and on her way home she spilled 4 times 2 quarts, less 3 quarts; how many quarts had she remaining?

77. Henry is 4 feet in height, and John is 5; and 5 times the sum of their heights, considered as a number, is equal to their father's age+15 years. Required, the father's age.

78. If an orange cost   cents, a lemon twice as much, and a melon 4 times as much as the orange and

lemon together, less 14 cents, how much r ore will 3 melons cost than 3 oranges and 3 lemons?

79. James has 9 walnuts, John twice as many less 8, and Joseph twice as many as James and John + 7; how many has each, and how many have all?

80. If an apple cost 2 cents, an orange three times as much less 4 cents, and a pine-apple three times as much as the apple and orange + 5 cents, what will be the cost of all three?

CHAPTER IV.

Lesson I.

1.   8   are   how   many   times   2 ?

SOLUTION.—8 are as many times 2 as 2 is contained times in 8, which are 4 times.

2.	6	are	how	many	times	2 ?
3.	4	are	how	many	times	2 ?
4.	10	are	how	many	times	2 ?
5.	12	are	how	many	times	2 ?
6.	14	are	how	many	times	2 ?
7.	6	are	how	many	times	3 ?
8.	9	are	how	many	times	3 ?
9.	12	are	how	many	times	3 ?
10.	15	are	how	many	times	3 ?
11.	18	are	how	many	times	3 ?
12.	21	are	how	many	times	3 ?
13.	24	are	how	many	times	3 ?
14.	16	are	how	many	times	2 ?
15.	18	are	how	many	times	2 ?
16.	20	are	how	many	times	2 ?
17.	22	are	how	many	times	2 ?
18.	24	are	how	many	times	2 ?
19.	26	are	how	many	times	2 ?
20.	28	are	how	many	times	4

21. At 2 cents apiece, how many apples can you buy for 4 cents?

SOLUTION.—If for 2 cents I can buy 1 apple, for 4 cents I can buy as many apples as 2 is contained times in 4, which are 2.

REMARK.—The following *solution* is preferred to the above, if the pupils are acquainted with *Fractions.*

SOLUTION.—If for 2 cents I can buy 1 apple, for 1 cent I can buy ½ of an apple; and for 4 cents, 4 times ½, which are ⁴⁄₂ or 2 apples.

22. At 2 cents apiece, how many oranges can I buy for 6 cents?

23. At 2 cents apiece, how many peaches can be bought for 8 cents?

24. At 3 dimes a yard, how many yards of calico can be bought for 12 dimes?

25. At 3 cents apiece, how many lemons can be bought for 9 cents?

26. At 2 cents a yard, how many yards of tape can be bought for 10 cents?

27. At 2 dimes a bushel, how many bushels of apples may be had for 12 dimes?

28. How many pounds of ginger, at 2 dimes a pound, may be had for 14 dimes?

29. How many baskets of strawberries, at 3 cents a basket, can be had for 15 cents?

30. For 16 dollars, how many yards of cloth can be had, at 2 dollars a yard?

31. For 18 apples, how many oranges can be bought, at the rate of 2 apples for 1 orange?

32. How many primers, at 2 cents apiece, can be bought for 24 cents?

33. How many barrels of flour, at 2 dollars a barr can be bought for 20 dollars?

34. For 22 dollars, how many sheep may be boug at 2 dollars apiece.

35. How many melons may be had for 18 dimes 3 dimes apiece?

36. At 3 cents apiece, how many tops may be had for 6 cents?

37. If 1 peck of beans cost 3 dimes, how many pecks can be bought for 21 dimes?

38. At 3 cents a mile, how many miles can I ride for 24 cents?

39. How many bushels of rye, at 4 dimes a bushel, may be bought for 12 dimes?

40. How many books, at 4 dimes each, can be bought for 20 dimes?

41. 8 are how many times 4?
42. 12 are how many times 4?
43. 16 are how many times 4?
44. 10 are how many times 5?
45. 15 are how many times 5?
46. 20 are how many times 5?
47. 28 are how many times 7?
48. 32 are how many times 4?
49. 30 are how many times 5?
50. 35 are how many times 5?
51. 36 are how many times 4?
52. 40 are how many times 5?
53. 44 are how many times 4?
54. 30 are how many times 6?
55. 48 contains 8 how many times?

SOLUTION.—48 contains 8, 6 times [because 6 times 8 are 48.]

56. 24 contains 8 how many times? 4? 12? 3?

57. 36 contains 9 how many times? 6? 3? 2?

58. 54 contains 2 how many times? 3? 9?

59. 75 contains 3 how many times? 5? 15?

60. 68 contains 2 how many times? 4?

61. At 5 dimes each, how many turkeys can be had for 25 dimes?

62. If the wages of 1 day is 4 dimes, what will be the wages for 9 days?

63. How many days will a man be required to work for 12 dimes, if he receive 4 dimes a day?

4

64. If a boy spends 5 cents a day, how many days will it take him to spend 15 cents?

65. A boy had 20 marbles, and divided them equally among his 5 brothers; how many did each receive?

66. A boy divided 28 cents equally among 4 poor women; how many cents did each receive?

67. A farmer gave 4 of his labourers 32 bushels of corn; how many bushels did each receive?

68. If 5 quarts af molasses cost 30 cents, what will 1 quart cost?

69. At 5 cents a yard, how many yards of ribbon may be had for 35 cents? how many for 50 cents?

70. How many pine-apples, at 8 cents each, can be obtained for 40 cents? for 56 cents?

71. If a man travel 45 miles in 9 hours, how many miles does he travel in 1 hour?

72. If a man travel 5 miles in an hour, how many hours will it take him to travel 40 miles?

73. How many yards of cloth, at 4 dollars a yard, can you buy for 32 dollars?

74. In a certain orchard there are 48 trees standing in rows, and 6 trees in each row; how many rows are there in the orchard?

75. For 56 dollars, how many barrels of pork can be bought, at 8 dollars a barrel?

76. If a man can travel 6 miles in an hour, how long will it take him to travel 42 miles?

77. How many yards of cloth, at 4 dollars a yard, can you buy for 36 dollars?

78. A butcher gave 39 dollars for sheep, at the rate of 3 dollars a head; how many sheep did he buy?

79. 45 dollars were given for 9 barrels of flour; how much was it a barrel?

80. How long would it take to travel 72 miles, at th. rate of 3 miles an hour?

Lesson II.

1. 20 are how many times 2? 4? 10?
2. 22 are how many times 11?
3. 24 are how many times 3? 4? 2?
4. 25 are how many times 5?
5. 28 are how many times 2? 7?
6. 30 are how many times 2? 3? 5?
7. 32 are how many times 2? 4? 16? 8?
8. 34 are how many times 17?
9. 40 are how many times 2? 4? 5? 8?
10. 44 are how many times 2? 11?
11. 46 are how many times 23?
12. 48 are how many times 2? 3? 4? 6?
13. 50 are how many times 2? 10?
14. 56 are how many times 2? 7?
15. 57 are how many times 3?
16. 60 are how many times 2? 3? 4? 5? 6?
17. 64 are how many times 2? 4? 8?
18. 66 are how many times 2? 3? 6?
19. 68 are how many times 2? 4?
20. 70 are how many times 10? 2?
21. 72 are how many times 2? 4? 6? 8?
22. 5 are how many times 2, and how many remaining?

REMARK.—Whenever there is a remainder, it may be mentioned simply as a remainder.

23. 7 are how many times 2?
24. 17 are how many times 4? 2? 5?
25. 18 are how many times 6? 4? 2?
26. 34 are how many times 4? 6? 5? 2?
27. 25 are how many times 5? 4? 2? 3?
28. 16 are how many times 9? 4? 8? 7?
29. 32 are how many times 7? 5? 6?
30. 63 are how many times 9? 4? 5? 6?
31. 74 are how many times 2? 4? 6? 7?

32. 80 are how many times 2? 3? 4? 5? 6? 7? 8?
33. 81 are how many times 2? 3? 4? 5? 6? 7? 8?
34. 15 are how many times 4? 6? 7? 8?
35. 29 are how many times 2? 3? 4? 5? 6? 7?
36. 90 are how many times 2? 4? 6? 8? 9? 11?
37. 144 are how many times 2? 4? 6? 8? 12?

Lesson III.

1. At 2 cents each, how many lemons can you buy for 14 cents?

SOLUTION.—If 1 lemon cost 2 cents, for 14 cents I can buy as many lemons as 2 is contained times in 14, which are 7.

ANOTHER SOLUTION.—If for 2 cents I can buy 1 lemon, for 1 cent I can buy 1 half of a lemon, and for 14 cents, 14 times 1 half, which are 14 halves, or 7 lemons.

2. How many boxes of cheese, at 4 dollars a box, may be had for 12 dollars?

3. If one hundred pounds of hay cost 3 dollars, how many hundred may be had for 15 dollars?

4. If 1 barrel of flour support 20 persons 1 week, how many persons will it support 4 weeks?

5. If 1 man can ride 1 mile for 4 cents, how far can 2 men ride for 80 cents?

6. If 10 men accomplish a certain piece of work in 2 days, how long will it take 1 man to do the same?

7. If 3 yards of cloth make 1 coat, how many coats will 18 yards make?

8. If I receive 12 dollars interest in 1 year, in how many years will I receive 144 dollars interest?

9. A man travelled 7 miles in 1 hour; at the same rate, how long would it take him to travel 63 miles?

10. If 1 cow cost 13 dollars, how many cows may be had for 65 dollars?

11. How many pens can you buy for 27 cents, if 1 pen cost 3 cents?

12. If 8 apples are worth 40 chestnuts, how many chestnuts is 1 apple worth?

13. How many cents is 1 lemon worth, if 12 lemons are worth 48 cents?

14. How much will 1 cord of wood cost, if 20 cords cost 40 dollars?

15. If 1 pound of beef cost 7 cents, how much will 19 pounds cost?

16. For 147 cents, how many pounds of sugar can be bought, at 7 cents a pound?

17. If 9 yards of cloth cost 53 dollars, for how much must it be sold a yard to gain 10 dollars?

18. If 7 barrels of flour cost 38 dollars, and were sold at 7 dollars a barrel, what was the gain?

19. How many peaches, at 4 cents each, may be bought for 96 cents?

20. How many yards of cloth, at 4 dollars a yard, can be bought for 116 dollars?

21. How many oranges, at 3 cents each, must be given for 18 lemons, worth 4 cents each?

22. If 15 sheep cost 75 dollars, what will 1 sheep cost?

23. Which will cost the most, 4 barrels of wheat flour, at 9 dollars a barrel, or 12 barrels of corn, at 4 dollars a barrel, and how much?

24. How many barrels of beef, at 3 dollars a barrel, can be bought for 54 dollars?

25. How many pounds of fish, at 5 cents a pound, may be had for 95 cents?

26. At 7 cents a pound, how many pounds of lead may be had for 84 cents?

27. How long will it require to travel 105 miles, at the rate of 5 miles an hour?

28. A person divided 72 peaches equally among 6 boys; how many did each receive?

29. 148 marbles were divided equally among some

boys; how many boys were there, provided each boy received 2 marbles?

30. How many pounds of butter, at 14 cents a pound, can be bought for 28 apples, at 3 cents each?

31. At 7 cents a bottle, how many bottles of ink can you buy for 14 sheets of paper, at 2 cents a sheet?

32. In how many days can 1 man do as much as 7 men in 8 days?

33. In how many days can 2 men do as much work as 6 men in 3 days?

34. In how many days can 4 men earn as much as 8 men in 6 days?

35. In how many days can 15 men earn as much as 3 men in 25 days?

36. In how many months will 6 horses eat as much as 18 horses in 5 months?

37. How many men can in 7 days earn as much as 28 men in 4 days?

38. In 10 days 6 men will earn as much as how many men in 5 days?

39. How many yards of cloth, at 4 dollars a yard, may be had for 4 sets of chairs, at 12 dollars a set?

40. A farmer gave 13 barrels of flour, worth 4 dollars a barrel, for 26 yards of cloth; how much was the cloth a yard?

Lesson IV.

CHAPTERS FIRST, SECOND, THIRD, AND FOURTH COMBINED.

1. 4 times 6 are how many times 2?

SOLUTION.—4 times 6 are 24.   24 are 12 times 2.   Therefore, 4 times 6 are 12 times 2.

2. 4 times 9 are how many times 3?

3. 4 times 8 are how many times 2?

4. 4 times 10 are how many times 5?
5. 4 times 12 are how many times 6?
6. 4 times 14 are how many times 7?
7. 5 times 9 are how many times 15?
8. 5 times 8 are how many times 4?
9. 5 times 12 are how many times 15? 6?
10. 6 times 7 are how many times 2?
11. 6 times 8 are how many times 12? 3?
12. 4 times 6 are how many times 8?
13. 7 times 15 are how many times 5?
14. 12 times 7 are how many times 21?
15. 8 times 7 are how many times 4?
16. How many times 12 are 9 times 4?
17. How many times 20 are 5 times 4?
18. How many times 9 are 3 times 21,+9?
19. How many times 5 are 7 times 15,+10—5?
20. How many times 9 are 3 times 36,—2+11?
21. How many times 12 are 9 times 4,+24—12?
22. How many times 21 are 9 times 14,+42?
23. How many times 7 are 3 times 14,+21—14?
24. How many times 5 are 8 times 10,+5—15?
25. How many times 5 are 10 times 6,+15+5?
26. How many times 5 are 6 times 15,+10+15?
27. 10 times 4,+2 are how many times 7? 2?
28. 8 times 9,—2 are how many times 5?
29. 12 times 8,—8 are how many times 2?
30. 26 times 11,—6 are how many times 28?
31. 7 times 8,+4 are how many times 12?
32. 6 times 7,+4 are how many times 2?
33. 5 times 8,+8 are how many times 6?
34. 4 times 9,—4 are how many times 8?
35. 9 times 5,—3 are how many times 7?
36. 7 times 12,—14+5 are how many times 5?
37. 4 times 15,+7—3 are how many times 8?
38. 6 times 7,+14—2 are how many times 9?
39. 11 times 13,+11—14 are how many times 7?
40. 11 times 15,—10+15 are how many times 17?

Lesson V.

PRACTICAL QUESTIONS COMBINING CHAPTERS THIRD AND FOURTH.

1. If 2 apples cost 4 cents, how much will 3 apples cost?

SOLUTION.—If 2 apples cost 4 cents, 1 apple will cost 1 half of 4 cents, which is 2 cents. If 1 apple cost 2 cents, 3 apples will cost 3 times 2 cents, which are 6 cents.

2. If 2 pears cost 16 cents, how much will 5 pears cost?

3. If 4 quinces cost 12 cents, how much will 3 quinces cost?

4. If 6 oranges cost 18 cents, how much will 9 oranges cost?

5. If 7 peaches cost 21 cents, how much will 9 peaches cost?

6. If 4 lemons cost 24 cents, how much will 7 lemons cost?

7. If 3 yards of tape cost 18 cents, how much will 6 yards cost?

8. If 7 hair-brushes cost 28 dimes, how many cents will 6 hair-brushes cost?

9. If 9 yards of muslin cost 108 cents, how much will 7 yards cost?

10. If 11 books cost 44 dimes, how many cents will 7 books cost?

11. If 12 ink-stands cost 96 cents, what will 2 cost?

12. If 10 lead-pencils cost 30 cents, how much will be the cost of 7? of 9? of 2? of 15? of 12?

13. How much will 13 yards of silk cost, if 5 yards cost 45 dimes?

14. If a man travel 15 miles in 3 hours, how far, at this rate, can he travel in 9 hours? 5 hours? 7 hours?

15. If the cartage of a load of plaster 20 miles cost 4 dollars, how far could it be carried for 12 dollars?

16. How many pair of pantaloons can be cut out of 21 yards of cloth, if 3 pair can be cut out of 9 yards of the same kind of cloth?

17. How much will 30 pounds of sugar cost, if 6 pounds cost 42 cents?

18. How much will 18 pounds of veal cost, if 6 pounds cost 42 cents?

19. How much will 75 pounds of pork cost, if 9 pounds cost 75 cents?

20. How much will 20 weeks' board amount to, if 7 weeks' board cost 14 dollars?

21. How much will be the wages for 1 year, if 4 months' wages amount to 48 dollars?

22. How much will be the cost of 25 bushels of apples, if 13 bushels cost 260 cents?

23. How much will 14 pounds of cheese cost, if 6 pounds cost 54 cents?

24. If 7 quarts of milk cost 35 cents, how much will 36 quarts cost?

25. If 4 men can do a certain piece of work in 12 days, in how many days will 3 men do the same work?

26. I gave 72 dollars for a quantity of cotton, and sold it for 12 yards of cloth; how much did the cloth cost me a yard?

27. Gave 15 pounds of sugar for 5 pounds of butter; how much did the butter cost a pound, provided 8 pounds of sugar were worth 56 cents?

28. If 4 chestnuts are worth 8 walnuts, how many walnuts are 27 chestnuts worth?

29. If 7 yards of broadcloth are worth 35 dollars, how many boxes of butter, at 3 dollars a box, would 9 yards of this cloth buy?

30. A man bought 4 barrels of flour for 20 dollars, and gave 3 of them for cider, at 3 dollars a barrel; how many barrels of cider did he get?

31. A man bought 14 barrels of cider for 56 dollars, and gave 5 barrels of it for cloth at 2 dollars a yard; how many yards did he receive?

32. A merchant having 15 yards of cloth worth 73

dollars, gave 10 of them for pork, worth 10 dollars a barrel; how many barrels did he receive?

33. When 9 bushels of rye were worth 45 dimes, 12 bushels were given for 15 yards of cloth; how much did the cloth cost a yard?

34. If 35 yards of cloth cost 140 dollars, how much will 95 yards of the same cloth cost?

35. Two boys are 32 rods apart, and both running in the same direction, the hindermost boy gains on the other 4 rods each minute; in how many minutes will he overtake him?

36. How many boxes will be required to contain 56 bushels, provided each box contains 8 bushels?

37. How many barrels of onions, at 3 dollars a barrel, must be given for 21 boxes of raisins, at 2 dollars a box?

38. A farmer bought 9 yards of cloth, at 4 dollars a yard, and paid for it with cider, at 3 dollars a barrel; how many barrels did he take?

39. How long would it take a man to lay up 24 dollars, if he save 2 dollars a week?

40. A farmer hired a laborer and agreed to give him 6 dollars for every 3 days' work; how much did he receive a week, allowing 6 working days in a week? how much a month, allowing 4 weeks to the month?

41. If 4 oranges are worth 12 cents, how many oranges must be given for 6 pine-apples, worth 12 cents each?

42. How many yards of cloth, at 2 dollars a yard, can be bought for 4 reams of paper, at 5 dollars a ream?

43. 6 men bought a horse for 80 dollars, and paid 2 dollars a week for keeping him;—at the end of 10 weeks they sold him for 82 dollars; how much did each man lose?

44. If 2 apples are worth 1 orange, and 2 oranges

are worth 1 lemon, how many lemons can be bought for 48 apples?

45. If 5 oranges are worth 1 pine-apple, and 2 pine-apples are worth 1 melon, how many oranges may be bought for 4 melons?

46. A fox is 80 rods before a hound, and the hound gains 5 rods on the fox every 10 minutes; in how many minutes will the fox be caught?

47. If 7 men can do a certain job of work in 12 days, in how many days could 21 men do the same work?

48. In how many days can 9 men do as much work as 7 men can in 18 days?

49. How many men in 10 days can perform the same amount of work that 8 men can in 5 days?

50. Bought 5 firkins of butter for 35 dollars; for what must I sell it to gain 10 dollars? what is the gain on each firkin?

CHAPTER V.

Lesson I.

TABLE OF UNITED STATES CURRENCY.

10 Mills *(m.)*	make 1 Cent,	marked *c.*
10 Cents	" 1 Dime,	" *d.*
10 Dimes	" 1 Dollar,	" $.
10 Dollars	" 1 Eagle,	" *E.*

1. How many mills in 4 cents?

Solution.—In 1 cent there are 10 mills, and in 4 cents there are 4 times 10 mills, or 40 mills.

2. How many mills in 3 cents? In 5 cents? In 8 cents?

3. How many cents in 2 dimes? In 4 dimes? In 5 dimes? In 6 dimes? In 9 dimes? In 10 dimes?

4. How many dimes in $1? In $2? In $3? In $4? In $5? In $6?

5. How many dimes in 1 eagle and $4? In 2 eagles and $8?

6. How many cents in $1? In $2? In $3? In $4? In $5? In $8?

7. How many dollars in 80 dimes?

SOLUTION.—There are 10 dimes in $1, therefore, I tenth of the number of dimes equals the number of dollars. 1 tenth of 80 is 8. Therefore, in 80 dimes there are $8.

8. How many dimes in 60 cents? In 70 cents? In 90 cents?

9. How many dollars in 200 cents? In 500 cents? In 800 cents? In 360 cents? In 705 cents?

10. If 3 yards of muslin cost 6 dimes, how many yards can be bought for 1 dollar?

11. How many pounds of pepper can you buy for 1 eagle, if 12 pounds cost 6 dimes?

12. How many pounds of candies can you buy for 14 eagles, if 10 pounds cost 140 cents?

Lesson II.

TABLE OF ENGLISH MONEY.

4 Farthings (far.)	make 1 Penny, marked d.
12 Pence	" 1 Shilling, " s.
20 Shillings	" 1 Pound, " £.

A Soverign (sov.) is equal in value to 1£.

1. How many shillings in 4£ 15 shillings.

SOLUTION.—There are 20 shillings in 1£, therefore 20 times the number of pounds equal the number of shillings. 20 times 4 are 80 shillings+15, are 95 shillings.

2. How many pence in 1 shilling? In 4 shillings? In 3 shillings? In 7 shillings? In 9 shillings?

3. How many shillings in 1£? In 2£? In 3£? In 6£?

4. How many pence in 2£ 10 shillings 5 pence?

5. How many pounds in 60 shillings? In 80s.? In 120s.?

6. How many pounds in 480 pence? In 720d.?

7. At 4 shillings a bushel, how many pounds will 40 bushels of potatoes cost?

8. At 10 pence apiece, how many pounds will 49 pine-apples cost?

9. At 5 shillings a yard, how many yards of cloth can be bought for 2£ 15 shillings?

Lesson III.

TABLE OF TROY WEIGHT.

24 Grains *(gr.)*   make 1 Pennyweight, marked *dwt.*
20 Pennyweights   " 1 Ounce,   " *oz.*
12 Ounces   " 1 Pound,   " *lb.*

1. How many pennyweights in 240 grains?

2. How many pennyweights in 4 ounces? In 5 ounces? In 6 ounces?

3. How many ounces in 1 pound? In 3 pounds? In 5 pounds? In 8 pounds?

4. In 24 ounces how many pounds? In 48 ounces? In 36 ounces? In 60 ounces? In 84 ounces?

5. How many ounces in 20 pennyweights? In 40? In 60? In 70?

6. If 7 grains of gold cost 168 dimes, how much will 10 pennyweights cost?

7. What will 1 pennyweight of gold cost, if 2 grains cost 18 dimes?

8. How many pennyweights in 4 ounces and 6 pennyweights?

9. How many pounds in 480 pennyweights?

10. How many grains in 2 oz., 2 dwt., and 2 gr.?

4

Lesson IV.

TABLE OF AVOIRDUPOIS WEIGHT.

16 Drams (*dr.*)	make I Ounce,	marked	*oz.*
16 Ounces	" 1 Pound,	"	*lb.*
25 Pounds	" 1 Quarter,	"	*qr.*
4 Quarters, or 100 lbs,	" 1 Hundred-weight,	"	*cwt.*
20 Hundred-weight,	" 1 Ton,	"	*T.*

1. How many drams in 2 oz.? In 4 oz.? In 10 oz.?

2. How many ounces in 2 lbs.? In 4 lbs.? In 8 lbs.?

3. How many quarters in 100 pounds? In 400 pounds? In 600 pounds? In 1200 pounds?

4. How many pounds in 3 qrs.? In 2 qrs.? In 7 qrs.?

5. How many quarters in 2 hundred-weight?

6. In 8 quarters how many hundred-weight?

7. If 30 lbs. of hay cost 6 dimes, what will 3 quarters cost? will 1 cwt.? will 2 cwt. and 1 qr.?

8. What will 2 tons of iron cost, if 1 lb. cost 1 dime?

9. What will 40 tons of hay cost, at 2 dimes a qr.?

10. What will 2 cwt. of sugar cost, at a dime a pound? at 5 cents a pound?

Lesson V.

TABLE OF LONG MEASURE.

12 Inches (*in.*)	make 1 Foot,	marked	*ft.*
3 Feet	" 1 Yard,	"	*yd.*
5½ Yards, or 16½ feet	" 1 Rod,	"	*rd.*
40 Rods	" 1 Furlong,	"	*fur.*
8 Furlongs, or 320 rods,	" 1 Mile,	"	*mi.*
3 Miles	" 1 League,	"	*lea.*
69½ Miles	" 1 Degree,	"	*deg.* or °.
360 Degrees	" 1 Circle of the Earth.		

1. How many inches in 1 ft.? In 2 ft.? In 4 ft.? In 5 ft.? In 10 ft.?

2. How many feet in 2 yds.? In 6 yds.? In 5 yds.?
In 12 yds.?

3. How many yards in 2 rods? In 4 rds.? In 8
rds.? In 10 rds.?

4. How many furlongs in 4 miles? In 6 mi.? In
9 mi.?

5. How many inches in 4 yds. 2 ft. 10 in.?

6. In 216 inches, how many yards? In 288 in.?

7. How many rods in 1 mile?

8. How many miles in 1760 yards?

9. How many feet in 2 rods, 3 yds., 2 ft., 11 in.?

10. How many feet in 1 mile?

Lesson VI.

TABLE OF CLOTH MEASURE.

2¼	inches	make	1	Nail,	marked	na.
4	Nails	"	1	Quarter of a yard,	"	qr.
4	Quarters	"	1	Yard	"	yd.
3	Quarters	"	1	Ell Flemish,	"	E. Fl.
5	Quarters	"	1	Ell English,	"	E. E.
6	Quarters	"	1	Ell French,	"	E. Fr

1. In 4 yds. 3 qrs., how many quarters?

2. In 7 yds. 2 qrs., how many Ells French?

3. In 3 yds. 3 qrs., how many Ells Flemish?

4. In 8 Ells English, how many yards?

5. In 7 Ells Flemish, how many yds. and quarters?

6. In 3 Ells French, how many yds. and quarters.

7. In 4 Ells Fr., and 8 Ells Fl., how many yards?

8. In 1 qr., how many inches?

9. What will 6 E.E. of cloth cost, if 6 nails cost 48
cents?

10. What will 3 E. E. + 2 E. Fr. of cloth cost, if 3
nails cost 12 cents?

Lesson VII.

TABLE OF LAND OR SQUARE MEASURE.

144 Square inches, (*sq. in.*)	make	1 Square foot,	*sq. ft*
9 Square feet	"	1 Square yard,	*sq. yd.*
30¼ Square yards	"	1 Square rod, or pole,	*P.*
40 Square rods	"	1 Rood,	*R.*
4 Roods	"	1 Acre,	*A.*
640 Acres	"	1 Square mile,	*sq. m.*

1. How many square feet in 4 sq. yds.? In 8 sq. yds.?

2. How many poles in 4 roods? In 6 roods?

3. How many acres in 40 roods? In 160 roods?

4. How many square yards in 81 sq. ft.? In 108 sq. ft.?

5. How many square yards in 1 rood 10 rods?

Lesson VIII.

TABLE OF CUBIC MEASURE.

1728 Cubic inches (*cu. in.*)	make	1 Cubic foot,	*cu. ft.*
27 Cubic feet	"	1 Cubic yard,	*cu. yd.*
24¾ Cubic feet	"	1 Perch of stone,	*pch.*
16 Cubic feet	"	1 Cord foot,	*c. ft.*
8 Cord feet, or 128 Cubic feet	"	1 Cord of wood,	*C.*

1. How many cubic feet in 4 cubic yards?

2. How many cubic feet in 4 perches of stone?

3. How many cords in 96 cord feet? In 72 c. ft.?

4. How many cords in 128 cu. ft.? In 384 cubic feet?

5. How many cord feet in 4 cords? In 6 cords? In 9 cords?

Lesson IX.

TABLE OF WINE MEASURE.

4 Gills (*gi*)	make 1 Pint,	marked	*pt.*
2 Pints	" 1 Quart,	"	*qt.*
4 Quarts	" 1 Gallon,	"	*gal.*
42 Gallons	" 1 Tierce,	"	*tier.*
31½ Gallons	" 1 Barrel,	"	*bar.*
2 Bar. or 63 Gallons	" 1 Hogshead,	"	*hhd.*
2 Hogsheads	" 1 Pipe,	"	*pi.*
2 Pipes	" 1 Tun,	"	*tun.*

1. How many gills in 3 pints? In 4 pints?
2. In 3 qts. how many gills?
3. In 12 gallons how many pints?
4. What will 5 gal. of rum cost, if 4 gi. cost 5 cents?
5. How many pints in 2 pipes?
6. A merchant bought a hogshead of molasses for 20 dollars, and sold it at the rate of 15 cents for 3 pints; how much did he gain by the bargain?
7. How much will a gallon of wine cost, if 7 gills cost 21 cents?
8. In 1 tierce, how many pints?
9. In 4 quarts and 2 pints, how many gills?
10. In 1 tun, how many gills?
11. In 1 barrel, how many pints?

Lesson X.

TABLE OF DRY MEASURE.

2 Pints	make 1 Quart	marked	*qt.*
8 Quarts	" 1 Peck,	"	*pk.*
4 Pecks	" 1 Bushel	"	*bu.*

1. In 1 peck, how many pints?
2. 2 pecks will fill how many pint measures?
3. In 3 pecks and 3 quarts how many pints?

5*

4. In 1 bushel and 3 pecks, how many quarts?

5. In 1 bushel, how many quarts? how many pints?

6. If 8 pints of nuts cost 24 cents, what will 3 pecks cost at the same rate?

7. A market woman bought 4 quarts of strawberries for 29 cents, and sold them at 5 cents a pint; how much did she gain?

8. A person sold 2 bushels and 1 peck of currants, at 2 cents a pint, and in payment received 1 bushel of gooseberries, at 4 cents a pint; how much remains due?

9. What will 5 quarts of wheat cost, if 1 bushel cost 128 cents?

10. A farmer sold 1 bu. 3 pk. and 1 pt. of clover-seed, at 640 cents a bushel, and in payment received 1 bu. 2 pk. and 3 qts. of grass-seed, at 320 cents a bus.; how much remains due?

Lesson XI.

TABLE OF TIME.

60 Seconds (*sec.*)	make 1 Minute,	marked	*m.*
60 Minutes	" 1 Hour,	"	*hr*
24 Hours	" 1 Day,	"	*d.*
7 Days	" 1 Week,	"	*w.*
4 Weeks	" 1 Month,	"	*mo.*
12 Calendar months	" 1 Year,	"	*yr.*
52 Weeks	" 1 Year,	"	*yr.*
365 Days	" 1 Common Year	"	*yr.*
366 Days	" 1 Leap Year,	"	*yr.*
100 Years	" 1 Century,	"	*C.*

The following table exhibits the divisions of the year, the names of the months, and the number of days in each.

Winter {	1st month,	January,	has	31 days.	
	2nd "	February,	"	28, in leap year 29.	
Spring. {	3rd "	March,	"	31 days.	
	4th "	April,	"	30 "	
	5th "	May,	"	31 "	
Summer. {	6th "	June,	"	30 "	
	7th "	July,	"	31 "	
	8th "	August,	"	31 "	
Autumn. {	9th "	September,	"	30 "	
	10th "	October,	"	31 "	
	11th "	November,	"	30 "	
Winter. {	12th "	December	"	31 "	

The following lines will help to remember the number of days in each month:

"Thirty days hath September,
April, June and November ;
All the rest have thirty-one,
Except February alone,
Which hath but twenty-eight in fine,
Till leap-year gives it twenty-nine."

☞ *In our calculations on interest we shall reckon* 30 *days to the month, and* 12 *months to the year, although not strictly accurate.*

1. In 2 hours, how many seconds ?

2. In 2 weeks and 5 days, how many days ?

3. In 48 hours, how many days?

4. 7200 seconds, how many hours ?

5. How many hours in a week ?

6. In 1 day, 12 hours and 10 minutes, how many minutes?

7. How many hours in a month ?

8. If a boy can do a piece of work in 40 minutes, how many hours would it take him to perform 12 times as much work?

9. If I can ⎯ a piece of work in 10 minutes, how many hours would it take to perform a piece of work 12 times as large?

10. How many days in 3 weeks and 5 days?

Lesson XII.

MISCELLANEOUS TABLE.

12 Units	make	1 Dozen.
12 Dozen	"	1 Gross.
12 Gross	"	1 Grct Gross.
20 Units	"	1 Score.
24 Sheets of Paper	"	1 Quire.
20 Quires	"	1 Ream.
56 Pounds	"	1 Bushel of Corn.
60 Pounds	"	1 Bushel of Wheat.
196 Pounds	"	1 Barrel of Flour.
200 Pounds	"	{ 1 Barrel of Beef, Pork, or Fish.

1. What will 2 reams of paper cost, at 15 cents a quire?

2. How many sheets of paper in 1 ream?

3. How many years in "3 score years and 10"?

4. How many units in a gross?

5. How many units in 6 dozen dozen?

6. How many units in half of a dozen dozen?

CHAPTER VI.

Lesson I.

1. John has 6 nuts, and Joel 1 half as many; how many has he?

SOLUTION.—If John has 6 nuts, and Joel 1 half as many, Joel must have 1 half of 6, or 3 nuts.

2. Mary had 4 dresses, and Rachel 1 half as many; how many had she?

3. Jacob is 8 years old, and John is 1 half as old; how old is John?

4. Moses having 2 marbles, gave 1 half of them to his brother; how many had he left?

5. If you divide 6 apples equally between 2 boys, what part of them will each have?

6. What is 1 half of 6?

7. How many halves in 1?

8. If an orange cost 8 cents, and a peach 1 half as much, what is the cost of the peach?

9. James had 12 cakes, and John 1 half as many; how many had John?

10. If 3 apples cost 6 cents, what part of 6 cents will one apple cost?

11. What is 1 third of 6.

12. What is 1 half of 8? 10? 12? 14? 16? 18? 20?

13. If 3 quarts of strawberries cost 18 cents, what part of 18 cents will 1 quart cost? What part of 18 cents will 2 quarts cost?

14. What is 1 third of 18? 1 half of 18?

15. If 4 pounds of raisins cost 8 dimes, what part of 8 dimes will 1 pound cost? 2 pounds? 3 pounds? 4 pounds? 5 pounds? 6 pounds?

16. What is 1 fourth of 8? of 12? of 16? of 20?

17. What is 1 fifth of 15? of 10? of 20? of 30?

18. If 1 fifth of 15 is 3, what is 2 fifths of 15? 3 fifths? 4 fifths? 6 fifths? 8 fifths?

19. What is 1 sixth of 12?

20. If 1 sixth of 12 is 2, what is 2 sixths of 12? 3 sixths? 4 sixths? 5 sixths? 7 sixths? 8 sixths?

21. What is 1 seventh of 21?

22. If 1 seventh of 21 is 3, what is 2 sevenths of 21? 3 sevenths? 4 sevenths,? 5 sevenths? 6 sevenths?

23. If 1 pound of candies cost 12 cents. what part

of a pound can you buy for 1 cent? for 2 cents? for 3 cents? for 5 cents? for 8 cents?

24. If a coat cost $20, and a pair of pantaloons 1 fourth as much, how much will the pantaloons cost?

25. If 7 barrels of cider cost $28, what part of $28 will 1 barrel cost? 4 barrels? 7 barrels? 5 barrels?

26. What is 1 seventh of $28? 2 sevenths of $28? 4 sevenths? 5 sevenths? 7 sevenths? 6 sevenths?

27. If 1 pound of cheese cost 6 cents, how much will 1 third of a pound cost? 2 thirds?

28. If 12 lemons cost 36 cents, what part of 36 cents will 1 lemon cost? 2 lemons? 4 lemons? 5 lemons? 8 lemons? 10 lemons? 9 lemons? 7 lemons?

29. What is 1 twelfth of 36? 2 twelfths of 36? 4 twelfths? 5 twelfths? 6 twelfths? 9 twelfths? 10 twelfths? 14 twelfths?

30. What do you understand by 1 third? 2 thirds?

ANSWER.—When a thing has been divided into three equal parts, 1 of these parts is called 1 *third,* and two of these parts are called 2 *thirds.*

31. What do you understand by 1 half?

32. What do you understand by 1 fourth? 2 fourths? 3 fourths?

33. What do you understand by 1 fifth? 2 fifths? 3 fifths? 4 fifths?

34. How many thirds make a whole one?

35. How many fourths in 1?

36. What do you understand by 2 sixths? 4 sixths?

37. What do you understand by 3 sevenths? 2 sevenths? 4 sevenths? 5 sevenths?

38. How many sixths in 1?

39. How many ninths in 1?

40. How many eighths in 1?

41. How many sevenths in 1?

42. How many tenths in 1?

43. How many twentieths in 1?

44. What do you understand by 7 twelfths? 6 twelfths? 9 twelfths? 8 twelfths?

45. James had 9 marbles, and Jacob had 2 thirds as many; how many had he?

SOLUTION.—If James has 9 marbles, and Jacob 2 thirds as many, he must have 2 thirds of 9 marbles. 1 third of 9 is 3, and 2 thirds are 2 times 3, which are 6 marbles, Jacob's number.

46. Mary bought 12 candies, and Sarah bought 2 thirds as many; how many did Sarah buy?

47. Rachel has 12 primers, Mary 3 fourths as many, and Anthony 2 thirds as many as Mary; how many have Mary and Anthony respectively?

48. Albert is 15 years old, and Ebenezer is 4 fifths as old; how old is he?

49. Augustus has 40 cents, and Augusta has 5 eighths as many; how many has she?

50. Morgan had 36 marbles, and gave 4 sixths of them to Martin; how many did he give to Martin, and how many had he left?

51. Moses has 24 fire-crackers, and Nathan has 7 sixths as many; how many has he?

52. Mifflin had 45 cents, and Matthew had 5 ninths as many; how many had he?

53. Dubois is 20 years old, and his father is 9 fifths as old; what is his father's age?

54. A farmer had 84 sheep, and a wolf killed 1 third of them; how many had he remaining?

55. In a certain school there are 12 girls and 7 fourths as many boys;—required the number of boys, and the number of boys and girls together.

56. In a certain recitation 36 questions were asked, and 1 ninth of them answered wrong; how many were correctly answered?

57. 4 fifths of all the words given out in a spelling lesson were spelled correctly, and 8 were misspelled; of how many words did the lesson consist?

58. Montgomery bought 9 filberts for 1 cent; what part of a cent did 1 cost? 2? 3? 6? 7? 9?

59. A horse was bought for $60, and sold for 7 fifths of what it cost; how much was the gain?

60. A received $140 for 14 weeks' labor, and paid 1 fifth of it for board? how much did he save each week?

61. How many are 4 fifths of 75?

62. How many are 7 eighths of 24?

63. Mr. A's wife is 40 years old, and 9 eighths of her age equals his; what is his age?

64. What is 2 ninths of 36? 4 ninths? 3 fourths? 4 sixths? 5 sixths? 4 twelfths? 9 twelfths?

65. How many are 3 fourths of 48? 4 sixths? 5 eighths? 7 eighths? 6 eighths? 5 sixths? 2 thirds?

66. 3 ninths of 27 are how many? 4 ninths? 7 ninths? 8 ninths? 2 thirds?

67. 3 fourths of 24 are how many times 3?

SOLUTION.—1 fourth of 24 is 6, and 3 fourths are 3 three times 6, or 18.   18 are 6 times 3.

68. 5 sevenths of 63 are how many times 3?

69. 3 eighths of 64 are how many times 6?

70. 9 thirds of 18 are how many times 3?

71. 4 fifths of 25 are how many times 2?

72. 6 ninths of 18 are how many times 6?

73. 7 ninths of 90 are how many times 2?

74. 4 thirds of 39 are how many times 2?

75. 15 seventeenths of 34 are how many times 6?

76. How many imes 17 are 17 eighteenths of 36?

77. How many times 8 are 12 thirteenths of 26?

78. How many times 5 are 10 thirds of 36?

79. How many times 4 are 2 thirds of 27,—2?

80. How many times 6 are 3 halves of 48, + 12?

81. Stephen having 40 apples, gave 3 fifths of them to one companion, and 3 eighths of them to another; how many had he remaining?

82. A had $120; 1 third of it he spent for a watch.

1 fourth of it for a suit of clothes, and 3 tenths of it for a sleigh; how much had he remaining?

83. Mr. B. being asked the cost of his hat, replied, 2 thirds of 30 dollars is 4 times its cost; required, the cost of the hat?

84. 14 ninths of $27 is equal to 7 times the cost of a pair of boots; required the cost of the boots.

85. An individual, having $90 on interest, received 2 forty-fifths of the principal for the interest, how much interest did he receive?

86. The interest received on $360 was 1 eighteenth of the principal; how much was the interest?

87. B. is worth $2,000, and 3 fourths of his fortune is 3 times A's; required A's fortune?

88. 3 eighths of the number of hours in a day is 3 times the number of hours I work; how many hours do I work?

89. A pole, whose length is 16 feet, is in the air and water; and 3 fourths of the whole length,—4 feet, equals the length in the air; required the length in the water.

90. 3 fifths of $2,000, + $120, equals B's fortune; how much is B worth?

91. The building of a certain house cost $560, and 4 sevenths of this, + $80, is 1 tenth of the cost of the farm on which it stands. Required the cost of the farm?

92. 5 eighths of 72, + 13, are how many times 2?

93. The interest on $960 for 5 years, was equal to 1 third of the principal; how much was the yearly interest?

94. What will 2 thirds of 12 pounds of coffee cost, at 13 cents a pound?

95. What will 3 fourths of a gallon of alcohol cost, at 9 cents a pint?

96. What will 1 sixteenth of a bushel of flax-seed cost, at 5 cents a pint?

97. How much will 7 fifteenths of 30 pine-apples cost at 2 dimes each?

98. How much will 7 ninths of a hogshead of molasses cost, at 4 dimes a gallon?

99. How many cents will 3 fifths of 100 oranges cost, at 1 half dime each?

100. If 1 pennyweight of gold cost $2, how much will 2 fifths of an ounce cost?

101. What will be the cost of 2 thirds of 36 pounds of butter, at 2 dimes a pound?

102. 2 thirds of 24, + 3 fourths of 16, are how many times 7?

103. 2 thirds of 30, + 3 fifths of 40, are how many times 8?

104. 3 sevenths of 21, + 3 eighths of 40, are how many times 6?

105. How far can I walk in 3 eighths of a day, at the rate of 3 miles an hour?

106. If Marcus earn 1 dime in an hour, how many cents can he earn in 3 eighths of a day?

107. If a horse travel 10 miles in an hour, how many times 10 miles can he travel in 5 twelfths of a day?

108. How many cents will 1 quart of gin cost, if 1 gill cost 15 mills?

109. How many dollars will 4 sixths of a pound of gold cost, if 1 pennyweight cost 12 dimes?

110. How many eagles will 25 fourths of a gallon of brandy cost, at 1 half dime a gill?

Lesson II.

1. If 1 third of an orange cost 2 cents, what will 1 orange cost?

SOLUTION.—If 1 third of an orange cost 2 cents, 3 thirds, or 1 orange, will cost 3 times 2 cents, which are 6 cents.

2. If 1 half of a pound of raisins cost 8 cents, what will 1 pound cost?

3. Bought 1 third of a barrel of sugar for $3; how much will 2 thirds of a barrel cost, at the same rate?

4. If 1 third of a pound of pork cost 5 cents, how much will 2 pounds cost?

5. 2 is 1 third of what number?

SOLUTION.—If 1 third of some number is 2, 3 thirds, which is that number, are 3 times 2, or 6.

6. 5 is 1 half of what number?

7. If 1 fourth of a lemon cost 2 cents, what will 1 cost?

8. If 1 fourth of a lemon cost 5 cents, what will 1 cost?

9. 3 is 1 fourth of what number?

10. 7 is 1 third of what number?

11. 12 is 1 fifth of what number?

12. 7 is 1 fourth of what number?

13. What will 4 fifths of a pound of cinnamon cost, if 1 fifth of a pound cost 5 cents?

14. If 1 fifth of a yard of cloth cost $2, what will a yard cost?

15. If 1 sixth of a gallon of vinegar cost 2 cents, what will 1 gallon cost?

16. A man, being asked the value of his horse, said that 1 eighth of its value is $12; what is the value of the horse?

17. A man gave 15 cents for his lodging, which was 1 seventh as much as his breakfast cost him; how much did he give for his breakfast?

18. Bought 1 eighth of a yard of cloth for 4 dimes; what will a yard cost at that rate?

19. If 1 tenth of a yard of cloth cost 47 cents, how much is that a yard?

20. What will 1 yard of cloth cost, if 1 ninth of a yard cost 5 cents?

21. What will 1 bushel of corn cost, if 1 seventh of a bushel cost 5 cents?

22. What will a hogshead of molasses cost, if 1 eighth of a hogshead cost $3.

23. What will be the cost of 2 cords of wood, if 1 eleventh of a cord cost 30 cents?

24. If 1 twelfth of the distance from Albany to Wilbraham is 9 miles, what is the entire distance?

25. 9 is 1 tenth of what number?

26. 15 is 1 seventh of what number?

27. 16 is 1 fifth of what number?

28. 12 is 1 fifth of 6 times what number?

29. 15 is 1 sixth of 5 times what number?

30. 18 is 1 fourth of 6 times what number?

31. 10 is 1 eighth of 20 times what number?

32. 15 is 1 seventh of 5 times what number?

33. 20 is 1 eighth of 16 times what number?

34. 30 is 1 third of 6 times what number?

35. A boy's hat cost $3, which was 1 fifth of the cost of his coat. The cost of the coat is required.

36. Mr. B's saddle cost $9, which was 1 fortieth of 6 times the cost of his horse. The cost of the horse is required.

37. Henry gave 5 cents for a piece of pie, which was 1 twentieth of 4 times as much as his breakfast cost him ; what was the cost of his breakfast?

38. A man, being asked his age, answered, that his youngest son's age, which was 12 years, was just 1 twelfth of 3 times his age. Required the father's age.

39. Mrs. B's shawl cost $9, which was 1 tenth of 3 times the cost of her dress; what was the cost of her dress?

40. John said to James, who is now 10 years old, your age is 1 eighth of 4 times my age. How old is John?

Lesson III.

1. If 2 thirds of a melon cost 4 cents, what will 1 melon cost?

SOLUTION.—If 2 thirds of a melon cost 4 cents, 1 third will cost 1 half of 4 cents, which is 2 cents, and 3 thirds, which is 1 melon, will cost 3 times 2 cents, which are 6 cents.

2. If 2 thirds of an orange cost 5 cents, what will 1 orange cost?

3. If 3 fourths of a pound of candies cost 9 cents, what will 1 pound cost?

4. If 4 thirds of a pound of spice cost 16 cents, what will 1 pound cost?

5. If 3 fourths of a pound of cinnamon cost 12 cents, what will 1 pound cost?

6. If $4 will buy 2 fifths of a barrel of fish, what will 1 fifth of a barrel cost?

7. What will 1 yard of cloth cost, if 4 sixths of a yard cost 120 cents.

8. What will 1 hogshead of molasses cost, if 5 sevenths of a hogshead cost $15.

9. 8 is 2 thirds of what number?

SOLUTION.—If 2 thirds of some number is 8, 1 third of that number is 1 half of 8, which is 4; and, 3 thirds, which is that number, are 3 times 4, which are 12. Therefore, 8 is 2 thirds of 12.

REMARK.—Representing the conditions and solutions of questions by symbols will aid young pupils in comprehending the more difficult parts of arithmetical analysis. Tho condition and analysis of the preceding question may be represented thus :—

1f ▨▨ $= \frac{2}{3}$ of some number $= 8$,

▨ $= \frac{1}{3}$ of that number $= 4$,

and ▨▨▨ $= \frac{3}{3}$, which is that number, $= 12$.

RE&
figure
and th
examp
the de
   The
parts t
of the
   1.
of th
   2.
1 of t
   3.
parts,
   4.
parts,
   5.
   6.
   7.
SOL
ber of
therefo

48. Reduce $\frac{15}{4}$ to a mixed number.
49. Reduce $\frac{12}{3}$ to a mixed number.
50. Reduce $\frac{23}{4}$ to a mixed number.
51. Reduce $\frac{21}{5}$ to a mixed number.
52. Reduce $\frac{57}{4}$ to a mixed number.
53. Reduce $\frac{89}{12}$ to a mixed number.
54. Reduce $\frac{94}{8}$ to a mixed number.
55. Reduce $\frac{25}{3}$ to a mixed number.
56. Reduce $\frac{37}{9}$ to a mixed number.
57. Reduce $\frac{47}{4}$ to a mixed number.
58. Reduce $\frac{78}{7}$ to a mixed number.
59. Reduce $\frac{37}{6}$ to a mixed number.
60. Reduce $\frac{34}{8}$ to a mixed number.

Lesson V.

1. James had $\frac{3}{4}$ of an apple, and John gave him $\frac{1}{4}$ more; how many had he then?

2. Mary had $\frac{5}{7}$ of an orange, and her father gave her $\frac{2}{7}$ of an orange more; how many had she then?

3. Robert had $\frac{2}{3}$ of a melon, and bought $\frac{2}{3}$ of another; how many had he then?

4. Susan had $\frac{5}{7}$ of a pint of walnuts, and gave $\frac{3}{7}$ of a pint to her sister; how much had she left?

5. James bought $\frac{19}{4}$ of a pound of candies, and on his way home ate $\frac{3}{4}$ of a pound; how much had he left?

6. John gave $\frac{1}{5}$ of a pound of raisins to James, $\frac{4}{5}$ of a pound to Mary, and kept $\frac{3}{5}$ of a pound himself; how much had he at first?

7. Mortimer gave $\frac{4}{5}$ of a dollar for a hat, $1\frac{2}{5}$ for a vest, and had $3\frac{4}{5}$ remaining; how much had he at first?

8. Jane had 5 pounds of cinnamon, and Harriet had $2\frac{3}{4}$ pounds; how many more had Jane than Harriet?

9. Henry gave $\frac{2}{3}$ of a dollar for his breakfast, $\frac{2}{5}$ of a
dollar for his dinner, and $\frac{4}{5}$ of a dollar for his supper;
how much did his day's board cost him?

10. $\frac{8}{9} + \frac{4}{9}$ are how many?

11. $\frac{7}{8} + \frac{6}{8}$ are how many?

12. $\frac{5}{8} + \frac{6}{8}$ are how many?

13. $\frac{9}{10} + \frac{8}{10}$ are how many?

14. $\frac{3}{4} + \frac{2}{4}$ are how many?

15. $1\frac{6}{3} + \frac{4}{3}$ are how many?

16. $1\frac{4}{3} + \frac{5}{3}$ are how many?

17. $1\frac{4}{8} + 1\frac{6}{8}$ are how many?

18. $\frac{9}{4} + 1\frac{3}{4}$ are how many?

19. $\frac{7}{8} + \frac{6}{8} + \frac{5}{8}$ are how many?

20. $\frac{3}{8} + \frac{6}{8} + \frac{4}{8}$ are how many?

21. $\frac{7}{10} + \frac{8}{10} + \frac{9}{10}$ are how many?

22. $\frac{2}{7} + \frac{4}{7} + \frac{6}{7}$ are how many?

23. $\frac{8}{9}$ less $\frac{4}{9}$ are how many ninths?

24. $2\frac{7}{8}$ less $1\frac{7}{8}$ are how many?

25. $1\frac{9}{4} - \frac{3}{4}$ are how many?

26. $2\frac{3}{3} - \frac{2}{3}$ are how many?

27. $3\frac{7}{5} - \frac{3}{5}$ are how many?

28. $1\frac{4}{3} - \frac{2}{3}$ are how many?

29. $3\frac{7}{8} - \frac{6}{8}$ are how many?

30. $1\frac{9}{7} - \frac{2}{7}$ are how many?

31. $4\frac{6}{9} - 1\frac{0}{9}$ are how many?

32. $4\frac{7}{8} - \frac{6}{8}$ are how many?

33. $5\frac{7}{12} - 3\frac{7}{12}$ are how many?

34. $\frac{9}{4} + \frac{7}{4} - \frac{3}{4}$ are how many?

35. $\frac{7}{8} + \frac{8}{8} - \frac{2}{8}$ are how many?

36. $\frac{4}{5} + 1\frac{7}{5} - \frac{9}{5}$ are how many?

37. $1\frac{4}{15} + 1\frac{0}{15} - 1\frac{2}{15}$ are how many?

38. $\frac{3}{5}$ of 60 $- \frac{3}{4}$ of 24 are how many?

39. $\frac{7}{8}$ of 40 $- \frac{2}{5}$ of 10 are how many?

40. $\frac{4}{5}$ of 15 $+ \frac{2}{3}$ of 9 $- \frac{3}{4}$ of 12 are how many?

Lesson VI.

1. At $\frac{2}{3}$ of a cent apiece what would 2 apples cost ·

SOLUTION.—If an apple cost $\frac{2}{3}$ of a cent, two apples will cost twice $\frac{2}{3}$ of a cent, which are $\frac{4}{3}$ or $1\frac{1}{3}$ cents.

2. At $\frac{2}{3}$ of a cent apiece, what will 5 apples cost?

3. At $\frac{1}{5}$ of a dime a pound, what will 10 pounds of candies cost?

4. At $1\frac{3}{4}$ dimes a pound, how many cents will 8 pounds of starch cost?

5. At $\frac{2}{5}$ of a cent apiece, what will 25 filberts cost?

6. At $\frac{8}{9}$ of a dime apiece, how many cents will 8 chickens cost?

7. At $\frac{2}{5}$ of a dollar a yard, what will 15 yards of linen cost?

8. If a man spend $\frac{3}{4}$ of a dollar a day, how much, at this rate, will he spend in 23 days?

9. If a man receive $\frac{2}{3}$ of an eagle in a week, how many dollars will he receive in 52 weeks?

10. If a pound of sugar cost $1\frac{1}{3}$ dime, what will 12 pounds cost?

11. At $5\frac{2}{3}$ cents a pound, what will 6 pounds of beef cost?

12. At $9\frac{3}{4}$ cents a pound, what will 8 pounds of pork cost?

13. At $6\frac{2}{5}$ cents each, what will 12 lemons cost? .

14. At $7\frac{3}{5}$ cents each, what will 20 rabbits cost?

15. At $12\frac{1}{2}$ cents a dozen, what will 4 dozen eggs cost?

16. At $11\frac{3}{8}$ cents a pound, what will 6 pounds of honey cost?

17. At $\$7\frac{1}{4}$ a bal. will 10 bals. tobacco cost?

18. At $\$9\frac{1}{4}$ a barrel, what will 10 bals. of pork cost?

19. What will 6 boxes of raisins cost, at $\$3\frac{2}{3}$ a box?

20. What will 14 bushels of wheat cost, at $1⅔ a bushel?

21. What will 7 barrels of cider cost, at $3¾ a barrel?

22. If a barrel of flour cost $4, what will 5¾ barrels cost?

23. 5 times 4 and $\frac{2}{4}$ of 4 are how many?

24. 7 times 6 and $\frac{4}{8}$ of 6 are how many?

25. 9 times 7 and $\frac{5}{7}$ of 7 are how many?

26. 12 times 9 and $\frac{8}{9}$ of 9 are how many?

27. 5 times 10 and $\frac{4}{5}$ of 10 are how many?

28. 13 times 4 and $\frac{3}{4}$ of 4 are how many? .

29. 8 times 7 and $\frac{3}{7}$ of 7 are how many?

30. 10 times 13 and $1\frac{1}{13}$ of 13 are how many?

31. 7 times 20 and $\frac{3}{5}$ of 20 are how many?

32. How many are 4 times $\frac{2}{3}$?

33. How many are 4 times $2\frac{2}{3}$?

34. How many are 3 times $4\frac{1}{2}$?

35. How many are 5 times $3\frac{1}{2}, + \frac{5}{7}$?

36. How many are 7 times $9\frac{2}{3}, + \frac{2}{3}$?

37. How many are 8 times $12\frac{5}{6}, - \frac{5}{6}$?

38. How many are 9 times $10\frac{3}{4}, - \frac{3}{4}$?

39. How many are 6 times $12\frac{2}{3}, + 2\frac{1}{3}$?

40. How many are 12 times $9\frac{7}{8}, + \frac{7}{8}$?

Lesson VII.

1. If you give to 6 persons, each $\frac{2}{3}$ of a dollar, how many dollars will be given?

2. What will be the cost of 4 yards of cloth, at $\frac{3}{4}$ of a dollar a yard?

3. If 1 yard of cloth cost $1⅔, what will 10 yards cost?

4. How many oranges will it require to give to each of 9 boys 1⅓ oranges?

5. How many barrels of flour does that man give away, who gives to each of 12 beggars $\frac{2}{3}$ of a barrel.

6. Anthony gave to each of his 7 companions $\frac{2}{5}$ of a pound of candies, and had $\frac{1}{3}$ of a pound left; how many pounds had he at first?

7. Thornton gave to each of 9 beggars $\frac{5}{8}$ of a dollar, and had $7 remaining; how much had he at first?

8. James gave $\frac{1}{12}$ of an orange to Jackson, $\frac{5}{12}$ to Joseph, and $\frac{2}{12}$ to John; what part of an orange had he remaining?

9. Harmon meeting 3 poor women and 5 poor men, gave to each woman $\frac{3}{8}$ of a dollar, and to each man $\frac{1}{8}$ of a dollar, and then had only $4 remaining; how much had he at first?

10. How many quarts of chestnuts must that boy have, who gives to each of 20 persons $\frac{7}{8}$ of a quart, and has 7 quarts remaining?

11. Mary, after giving to each of her 12 companions as many pinks as she had roses, which were 2, had no flowers remaining but her roses.   How many flowers had she at first?

12. What will 1 quart of vinegar cost, if 1 pint cost $\frac{2}{3}$ of a cent?

13. If 1 gill of molasses cost $\frac{3}{5}$ of a cent, what will 2 quarts cost?

14. If 2 pints of beans cost 4 cents, what will 1 peck cost?

15. If 3 pecks of buckwheat cost 96 cents, what will 1 pint cost?

16. What will 10 yards of silesia cost, if 1 yard cost $18\frac{2}{5}$ cents.

17. How many cents will $4\frac{2}{3}$ yards of silk cost, if 1 yard cost 6 dimes?

18. What will $\frac{3}{5}$ of a yard of muslin cost, if 1 yard cost 10 cents?

19. What will 7 spools of thread cost, if 1 spool cost $7\frac{5}{8}$ cents?

20. What will $8\frac{2}{3}$ yards of silk cord cost, at 6 cents a yd?

21. If 1 yard of wadding cost 5 cents, what will $9\frac{4}{5}$ yards cost?

22. What will $6\frac{3}{4}$ yards of muslin cost, if 1 yard cost 8 cents?

23. What will $8\frac{3}{5}$ pounds of veal cost, at 5 cents a pound?

24. How much will $9\frac{3}{4}$ barrels of cider cost, at $4 a barrel?

25. What will 12 hats cost, at $3\frac{3}{4}$ each?

26. What will $5\frac{3}{4}$ yards of gingham cost, at 4 dimes a yard?

27. What will be the cost of 13 yards of bishop lawn, at $1\frac{4}{13}$ a yard?

28. What will be the cost of 8 looking-glasses, at $15\frac{3}{4}$ apiece?

29. What amount of money will be required to purchase 30 pounds of rice, at $6\frac{2}{5}$ cents a pound?

30. What will be the cost of 23 pounds of crackers, at $8\frac{1}{4}$ cents a pound?

31. What will 9 barrels of fish cost, at $12\frac{2}{3}$ a barrel?

32. If 1 grain of gold cost $9\frac{1}{2}$ dimes, what will 1 pennyweight cost?

33. If 1 gold pen cost $2\frac{2}{3}$ how much will 6 cost?

34. How many pounds of meat, at 5 cents a pound, can you buy for $3\frac{3}{5}$?

35. What will be the cost of 3 quarts of nuts, at 64 cents a peck?

36. If a coachman charge $5\frac{1}{2}$ cents a mile, how much must that man pay who rides 12 miles?

37. How many dollars, dimes, and cents will 12 yards of cloth cost, at 62 cents a yard?

38. How many dollars and cents will 4 pecks of grain seed cost, if 1 pint cost 5 cents?

39. How much will 13 yards of shalloon cost, at $13\frac{3}{4}$ cents a yard?

40. How many cents will 16 bushels of potatoes cost, at $2\frac{5}{8}$ dimes a bushel?

Lesson VIII.

☞ REMARK.—A fraction may be multiplied, by *multiplying* the *numerator* (as you have already observed), or by *dividing* the *denominator*.

1. How many are 5 times $\frac{7}{10}$?

SOLUTION.—5 times $\frac{7}{10}$ are $\frac{35}{10}$, or $3\frac{1}{2}$.

REMARK.—In accordance with the above remark we have

SOLUTION.—5 times $\frac{7}{10}$ are $\frac{7}{2}$, or $3\frac{1}{2}$.

2. How many are 3 times $\frac{13}{9}$?
3. How many are 9 times $\frac{6}{27}$?
4. How many are 5 times $\frac{27}{15}$?
5. How many are 6 times $\frac{27}{12}$?
6. How many are 9 times $\frac{4}{18}$?
7. How many are 9 times $\frac{16}{36}$?
8. How many are 7 times $\frac{39}{21}$?
9. 8 times $\frac{13}{16}$ are how many?
10. 11 times $\frac{13}{22}$ are how many?
11. 12 times $\frac{15}{28}$ are how many?
12. 2 times $\frac{9}{4}$ are how many?
13. 5 times $\frac{17}{20}$ are how many?
14. 6 times $\frac{49}{17}$ are how many?
15. 7 times $\frac{37}{14}$ are how many?
16. 12 times $\frac{13}{30}$ are how many?
17. How many times 5 are 8 times $\frac{40}{18}$?
18. How many times 12 are 9 times $\frac{48}{18}$?
19. How many times 8 are 11 times $\frac{64}{22}$?
20. How many times 100 are 25 times $\frac{400}{50}$?
21. How many times 20 are 35 times $\frac{800}{70}$?
22. 5 times $\frac{48}{5}$ is 4 times Mary's age; what is her age?

23. 13 times $\frac{150}{39}$ equals $\frac{1}{2}$ of the number of dollars a certain wagon cost. Required the cost of the wagon.

24. 25 times $\frac{100}{25}$ equals $\frac{1}{200}$ of the number of men Gen. Santa Anna had at the battle of Buena Vista. How many men had he?

25. 6 times $\frac{200}{12}$ is $\frac{1}{15}$ of the number of men he had wounded. How many men were wounded?

26. 7 times $\frac{560}{14}$ is $\frac{1}{4}$ of the number of men he had killed. How many were killed?

27. 4 times $\frac{450}{8}$ is $\frac{1}{20}$ of the number of men Gen. Taylor had. How many had he?

28. 9 times $\frac{67}{9}$ is $\frac{1}{4}$ of the number of men he had killed. How many were killed?

29. 8 times $\frac{15}{16}$ is $\frac{1}{2}$ of how many times 3?

30. 4 times $\frac{25}{12}$ is $\frac{1}{3}$ of how many times 5?

31. A laborer worked 12 months at the rate of $10\frac{3}{4}$ a month; how much did his year's wages amount to?

32. If 2 quarts of wine cost 48 cents, what will 1 gill cost?

33. How much ought I to pay for 3 oranges, at $\frac{3}{4}$ of a cent apiece?

34. If a certain piece of work can be performed in 96 hours, how many days will be required to perform it by working 6 hours a day?

35. If 1 man can dig a ditch in 15 days, how long will it take 5 men to dig it?

36. If a certain quantity of provisions serve a family of 4 persons 16 days, how long would it last a family of 8 persons?

37. If 8 men can perform a certain piece of work in 56 days, in how many days can 112 men do the same?

38. If 3 men can plow 18 acres in 6 days, in how many days could 9 men do the same?

39. 4 men can mow a certain field in $6\frac{1}{4}$ days; in how many days can five men perform the same work?

40. A man bought 6 barrels of cider, at \$$3\frac{2}{3}$ a barrel; how many boxes of butter, at \$4 a box, will it take to pay for it?

41. A merchant bought 6 yards of cloth, and sold it for \$20, which was $\frac{10}{9}$ of what it cost; what did it cost a yard?

42. Bought 36 yards of cloth, and sold $\frac{5}{9}$ of it for \$25, which was $\frac{5}{4}$ of what it cost; how much would I have gained by selling the whole at the same rate?

43. 7 men in $\frac{5}{7}$ of a day can earn \$10; how long would it take 1 man to earn the same?

44. James is $3\frac{3}{5}$ years of age, which is $\frac{1}{5}$ of the age of Henry; and Henry is 9 times as old as George. What is the age of Henry and of George respectively?

45. $\frac{1}{3}$ of 36 is 3 times $\frac{1}{2}$ of what number?

46. $\frac{1}{2}$ of 32 is $\frac{2}{3}$ of 3 times what number?

47. $\frac{2}{3}$ of 60 is $\frac{3}{5}$ of twice what number?

48. $\frac{3}{4}$ of 40 is $\frac{3}{7}$ of as many dollars as Mr. B's horse cost; what was the cost of his horse?

49. A person, being asked his age, said, that $\frac{3}{4}$ of 80 was $\frac{2}{3}$ of ten times his age. What was his age?

50. Morgan is 20 years old, and $\frac{1}{5}$ of his age is $\frac{4}{7}$ of the age of his brother. What was his brother's age?

Lesson IX.

1. How many thirds are there in 3?

SOLUTION.—In 1 there are 3 thirds, and in 3 there are 3 times 3 thirds, which are $\frac{9}{3}$.

The following solution is preferred to the above:

SOLUTION.—In 1 there are 3 thirds; therefore, 3 times the number of whole ones equal the number of thirds. 3 times 3 are 9; therefore, in 3 there are $\frac{9}{3}$.

2. How many fourths are there in 3?

3. How many halves are there in 6?

4. How many fifths are there in 4? in 5?
5. How many fifths are there in 7? in 8?
6. How many sixths are there in 4? in 3? in 5?
7. How many sevenths are there in 2? in 4? in 6?
8. How many eighths are there in 7? in 4? in 5?
9. How many fifteenths are there in 2? in 3? in 6?
10. How many tenths are there in 4? in 6? in 7?
11. How many fourths are there in 3 and $\frac{2}{4}$?
12. How many thirds are there in 4? and $\frac{1}{3}$?
13. How many thirds are there in 3 and $\frac{2}{3}$?
14. How many halves are there in 8 and $\frac{1}{2}$?
15. Reduce $6\frac{5}{6}$ to an improper fraction?
16. Reduce $9\frac{2}{5}$ to an improper fraction?
17. Reduce $7\frac{3}{4}$ to an improper fraction?
18. Reduce $5\frac{3}{4}$ to an improper fraction?
19. Reduce $4\frac{2}{3}$ to an improper fraction?
20. Among how many men can $5\frac{3}{7}$ bushels of wheat be distributed, provided each receives $\frac{1}{7}$ of a bushel?
21. Among how many boys can $7\frac{2}{8}$ oranges be divided, provided each receives $\frac{1}{8}$ of an orange?
22. 8 and $\frac{2}{9}$ are how many times $\frac{2}{9}$?

SOLUTION.—8 and $\frac{2}{9}$ equal $\frac{74}{9}$. $\frac{2}{9}$ is contained in $\frac{74}{9}$ 37 times.

23. $9\frac{6}{8}$ are how many times $\frac{2}{8}$?
24. $9\frac{3}{5}$ are how many times $\frac{3}{5}$?
25. $7\frac{4}{5}$ are how many times $\frac{3}{5}$?
26. $12\frac{2}{9}$ are how many times $\frac{5}{9}$?
27. $7\frac{5}{7}$ are how many times $\frac{3}{7}$?
28. $7\frac{2}{4}$ are how many times $\frac{3}{4}$?
29. $4\frac{3}{6}$ are how many times $\frac{9}{6}$?
30. $10\frac{4}{5}$ are how many times $\frac{3}{5}$?
31. $8\frac{6}{9}$ are how many times $\frac{3}{9}$?
32. $12\frac{6}{7}$ are how many times $\frac{3}{7}$?
33. 4 times $3\frac{1}{3}$ are how many times $\frac{2}{3}$?
34. 9 times $1\frac{3}{8}$ are how many times $\frac{4}{8}$?
35. 5 times $6\frac{2}{5}$ are how many times $\frac{2}{5}$?

36. 8 times $8\frac{2}{3}$ are how many times $\frac{2}{3}$?

37. 6 times $2\frac{1}{7}$ are how many times $\frac{3}{7}$?

38. A boy distributed $9\frac{3}{5}$ apples equally among his companions, giving to each $\frac{4}{5}$ of an apple; how many companions had he?

39. Homer distributed $\$12\frac{4}{5}$ equally among some poor women, giving to each $\$1\frac{3}{5}$; how many women were there?

40. Mary gave $\frac{3}{5}$ of a pie to each of her 9 visitors; how many pies did it take?

41. Bought 8 yards of cloth, at $\$5\frac{2}{3}$ a yard; how many yards of silk, worth $\$1\frac{1}{3}$ a yard, will it take to pay for it?

42. Bought 9 yards of cloth, worth $\$1\frac{5}{6}$ a yard, and paid for it with raisins, at $\$1\frac{3}{6}$ a box; how many boxes did it take?

43. How many bushels of turnips, at $\$\frac{2}{5}$ a bushel, can be bought for 8 bushels of apples, at $\$\frac{3}{5}$ a bushel?

44. How many apples, at $\frac{3}{4}$ of a cent each, can be bought for 6 oranges, at $2\frac{1}{4}$ cents apiece?

45. How many yards of cloth, at $\$\frac{5}{7}$ a yard, can be bought for 10 boxes of butter, at $\$5\frac{3}{7}$ a box?

46. How many geese, at $\$\frac{7}{8}$ each, can be bought for 14 ducks, at $\$\frac{3}{8}$ apiece?

47. How many boxes of cheese, worth $\$2\frac{3}{7}$ a box, may be had for 17 boxes of butter, at $\$1\frac{3}{7}$ a box?

48. How many barrels of flour, worth $\$5\frac{2}{3}$ a barrel, may be had for 17 bunches of cotton, at $\$1\frac{1}{3}$ a bunch?

49. How many sheep, at $\$1\frac{1}{3}$ a head, may be had for 8 calves, at $\$3^{2}$ each?

50. How many quarts of alcohol, at $\frac{2}{3}$ of a cent a pint, may be had for 12 quarts of molasses, at $4\frac{1}{3}$ cents a quart?

51. Mary and Jane together picked 5 times $2\frac{2}{15}$ quarts of strawberries, and shared them equally with their companions; how many companions had each, provided each received $1\frac{1}{5}$ quarts?

Lesson X.

LESSONS NINTH AND TENTH COMBINED.

REMARKS.—A fraction may be divided by *multiplying the denominator*, or by *dividing the numerator*.

1. If 2 yards of cloth cost $\frac{4}{5}$, what will one yard cost?

SOLUTION.—If 2 yards cost $\frac{4}{5}$ of a dollar, 1 yard will cost $\frac{1}{2}$ of $\frac{4}{5}$ of a dollar, which is $\frac{2}{5}$ of a dollar.

2. If 3 apples cost $\frac{6}{7}$ of a cent, what will 1 apple cost?

3. If 2 oranges cost $\frac{6}{7}$ of a cent, what will 1 orange cost?

4. If 3 yards of cord cost $1\frac{2}{3}$ of a cent, what will 1 yard cost?

5. If 2 pounds of sugar cost $8\frac{2}{3}$, (or $\frac{26}{3}$ cents,) what will 1 pound cost?

6. If 2 pine-apples cost $14\frac{2}{3}$ cents, what will 1 pine-apple cost?

7. If $\frac{2}{3}$ of a melon is worth 2 oranges, how much is 1 orange worth?

8. If 3 apples are worth $2\frac{2}{7}$ quinces, what is 1 apple worth?

9. How many times 7 are $2\frac{1}{2}\frac{1}{3}$?

10. How many times 13 are $7\frac{4}{5}$?

11. How many times 7 are $9\frac{1}{3}$?

12. How many times 21 are $16\frac{4}{5}$?

13. How many times 8 are $33\frac{2}{3}$?

14. How many times 7 are $10\frac{1}{2}$?

15. How many times 11 are $40\frac{1}{3}$?

16. How many times 18 are $14\frac{2}{5}$?

17. How many times 3 are $4\frac{4}{1}$?

18. How many times 9 are $7\frac{5}{7}$?

19. How many times 6 are $9\frac{6}{8}$?

20. How many times 15 are $33\frac{1}{3}$?

6

21. If 9 oranges are worth $\$\frac{9}{10}$, how many cents is 1 orange worth?

22. If 4 boxes of figs cost $\frac{4}{5}$ of an eagle, how many dollars will 1 box cost?

23. If 7 pounds of cheese cost $\$\frac{7}{10}$, how many cents will 1 pound cost?

24. If 3 cakes cost $\frac{9}{10}$ of a dime, how many cents will 1 cake cost?

25. If 4 pounds of chocolate cost $4\frac{4}{5}$ of a dime, how many cents is that a·pound?

26. What will 1 portfolio cost, if 3 cost $\frac{9}{10}$ of an eagle?

27. If 8 quarts of alcohol cost 32 dimes, how many cents will two gills cost?

28. What will 1 pound of sugar cost, if 4 pounds cost $18\frac{2}{3}$ cents?

29. If 6 pounds of cheese cost $31\frac{3}{4}$ cents, what will 1 pound cost?

30. If 12 eggs cost $9\frac{3}{5}$ cents, what will be the cost of 1 egg?

31. If 7 yards of cloth cost $\$24\frac{1}{2}$, what will 1 yard cost?

32. If 5 silk shawls cost $\$27\frac{1}{2}$, how much is that apiece?

33. If 9 pair of boots cost $\$32\frac{2}{5}$; how much is that a pair?

34. If 9 oranges are worth $30\frac{3}{5}$ walnuts, how many walnuts is 1 orange worth?

35. A boy gave 8 apples for $18\frac{3}{3}$ marbles; how many marbles did he get for 1 apple?

36. A boy gave 7 cents for $17\frac{1}{2}$ crackers; how many did he get for 1 cent?

37. Mary gave 10 pins for $23\frac{1}{3}$ chestnuts; how many did she get for 1 pin?

38. If 3 yards of broadcloth are worth $18\frac{4}{9}$ yards of muslin, how many yards of muslin may be had for 1 yard of broadcloth?

39. If John can walk 13 miles while Josiah is walking $32\frac{1}{2}$ miles, how far can Josiah walk while John is walking 1 mile?

40. If two chestnuts are worth $\frac{2}{10}$ of a cent, and 20 chestnuts are worth $\frac{2}{7}$ of a lemon, how many cents is 1 lemon worth?

41. If 2 oranges cost $\frac{5}{3}$ of a cent, what will 1 orange cost?

SOLUTION.—If 2 oranges cost $\frac{5}{3}$ of a cent, 1 orange will cost $\frac{1}{2}$ of $\frac{5}{3}$ of a cent, which is $\frac{5}{6}$ of a cent.

42. If three yards of linen cost $\$1\frac{3}{5}$, what will 1 yard cost?

43. If 7 yards of tape cost $13\frac{2}{3}$ cents; what will 1 yard cost?

44. If 2 pints of molasses cost $1\frac{2}{5}$ dimes, how many cents will 1 gallon cost?

45. How many times 8 are $6\frac{1}{4}$?

46. How many times 6 are $5\frac{2}{3}$?

47. How many times 4 are $4\frac{1}{2}$?

48. How many times 2 are $13\frac{1}{3}$?

49. How many times 7 are $7\frac{3}{6}$?

50. How many times 8 are 9 times $\frac{27}{18}$?

51. How many times 3 are 6 times $1\frac{11}{18}$?

SOLUTION.—$1\frac{11}{18}$ equals $\frac{29}{18}$. 6 times $\frac{29}{18}$ are $\frac{29}{3}$. 3 is contained in $\frac{29}{3}$ $\frac{29}{9}$, or $3\frac{2}{9}$ times.

52. How many times 9 are 10 times $2\frac{3}{20}$?

53. How many times 7 are 5 times $3\frac{1}{10}$?

54. How many times 5 are 15 times $3\frac{7}{30}$?

55. How many times 7 are 15 times $1\frac{28}{45}$?

56. How many times 5 are 3 times $2\frac{2}{6}$?

57. How many times 6 are 4 times $5\frac{2}{6}$?

58. If $1\frac{2}{3}$ yards of cloth are worth $\$2\frac{1}{2}$, what is 1 yard worth?

59. If $6\frac{2}{3}$ bunches of grapes are worth 40 cents, how many cents is 1 bunch worth?

60. If $3\frac{2}{3}$ baskets of peaches are worth $\$5\frac{1}{2}$, what is 1 basket of peaches worth?

Lesson XI.

1. What is $\frac{1}{3}$ of 2?

SOLUTION.—$\frac{1}{3}$ of 1 is $\frac{1}{3}$; and, if $\frac{1}{3}$ of 1 is $\frac{1}{3}$, $\frac{1}{3}$ of 2 is twice $\frac{1}{3}$, which are $\frac{2}{3}$. Therefore $\frac{1}{3}$ of 2 is $\frac{2}{3}$ of 1.

2. What is $\frac{1}{3}$ of 4? of 8?
3. What is $\frac{1}{4}$ of 2? 3? 5? 7? 9?
4. What is $\frac{1}{3}$ of 3? 5? 7? 9? 11?
5. What is $\frac{1}{5}$ of 2? 3? 4? 7? 8?
6. What is $\frac{1}{6}$ of 2? 3? 5? 7? 9?
7. What is $\frac{1}{7}$ of 2? 3? 5? 4? 6? 9? 11?
8. What is $\frac{1}{8}$ of 2? 4? 3? 5? 6? 7? 9?
9. What is $\frac{1}{9}$ of 2? 4? 7? 6? 3? 12? 11?
10. What is $\frac{1}{10}$ of 7? 2? 4? 6? 9? 14? 15?
11. If 2 apples cost 3 cents, what will 1 apple cost?

SOLUTION.—If 2 apples cost 3 cents, 1 apple will cost $\frac{1}{2}$ of 3 cents, which is $\frac{3}{2}$, or $1\frac{1}{2}$ cents.

12 If 2 apples cost 5 cents, what will 1 apple cost?

13. If 3 pens cost 8 cents, what will 1 pen cost?

14. If 3 yards of tape cost 14 cents, what will 1 yard cost?

15. If 5 barrels of flour cost $21, what will 1 barrel cost?

16. If 7 pecks of dried apples cost 23 dimes, what will 1 peck cost?

17. If 4 chickens cost 9 dimes, what will 1 chicken cost?

18. What will 1 pound of tamarinds cost, if 6 pounds cost 27 dimes?

19. What will 1 barrel of flour cost, if 3 barrels cost $25?

20. If you divide 7 bushels of wheat, equally, among 5 persons, how much will each receive?

21. Joshua had 13 marbles, and Lewis had $\frac{1}{2}$ many + $\frac{1}{2}$ of a marble; how many had he?

22. A man divided 3 barrels of flour equally among 11 families; what part of a barrel did each receive?

23. A farmer divided 5 bushels of rye, equally, among 7 of his poor neighbors; what part of a bushel did he give to each?

24. Calvin had 4 pints of nuts, and shared them, equally, with 7 of his companions; how much did each receive?

25. Margaret, having 7 quarts of raspberries, shared them equally with 8 of her playmates; what part of a quart did each receive?

26. What will 1 pound of prunes cost, if 5 pounds cost 48 dimes?

27. What will 2 boxes of figs cost, if 7 boxes cost 29 dimes?

28. What will 4 quarts of strawberries cost, if 9 quarts cost 7 dimes?

29. What is $\frac{1}{3}$ of 2?

30. If $\frac{1}{3}$ of 2 is $\frac{2}{3}$, what is $\frac{2}{3}$ of 2?

31. What is $\frac{2}{3}$ of 5?

SOLUTION.—$\frac{1}{3}$ of 5 is $\frac{5}{3}$, and $\frac{2}{3}$ are 2 times $\frac{5}{3}$, which are $\frac{10}{3}$, or $3\frac{1}{3}$.

32. What is $\frac{3}{4}$ of 3? of 5? 6? 7? 9? 11?

33. What is $\frac{3}{5}$ of 2? of 3? 4? 9? 11? 13?

34. What is $\frac{5}{6}$ of 2? of 3? 5? 7? 9? 12? 20?

35. What is $\frac{4}{7}$ of 3? of 5? 8? 9? 15?

36. What is $\frac{7}{9}$ of 4? of 6? 8? 12? 11? 17?

37. What is $\frac{3}{8}$ of 3? of 5? 6? 9? 10? 15?

38. What is $\frac{7}{11}$ of 2? of 4? 5? 6? 10? 12?

39. What is $\frac{5}{12}$ of 2? of 4? 3? 9? 15? 21?

40. What is $\frac{7}{10}$ of 7? of 8? 9? 12? 15? 25?

41. How many cents will $\frac{2}{3}$ of a pound of candies cost, if 1 pound cost 2 dimes?

42. What will be the cost of $\frac{3}{4}$ of a box of raisins, if 1 box cost $3?

43. What will be the cost of $\frac{3}{5}$ of a yard of cloth, at 7 dimes a yard?

44. If a ton of hay cost $10, what will $2\frac{2}{3}$ tons cost?

45. Jeremiah is 91 years old, and $\frac{3}{7}$ of his age equals the age of his eldest son; how old is he?

46. Bought 21 yards of cloth for $48; but, being damaged, I sold $\frac{3}{4}$ of it at $1\frac{5}{8}$ a yard, and the remainder for what it cost. How much did I lose?

47. Bought 14 yards of cloth, and sold $\frac{3}{7}$ of it at $2 a yard, which amounted to $2 less than the whole piece cost. What did it cost a yard?

48. A horse was sold for $97, which was $1\frac{2}{7}$ times as much as it cost? What did tho horse cost?

49. If 9 yards of cloth cost $17, what will 3 yards cost?

50. If 6 yards of cloth cost $25, what will 9 yards cost?

51. What will 2 pounds of opium cost, if 5 pounds cost $42?

52. If 5 pounds of Indigo cost $32, what will 2 pounds cost?

53. A wagon was sold for $90, which was $\frac{5}{4}$ of what it cost. How much did it cost?

54. Two men started from the same place, and travelled the same way; one at the rate of 92 miles in 10 hours; the other at tho rate of $\frac{1}{10}$ miles in $\frac{1}{7}$ of an hour; how far apart will they be in 2 hours?

55. By a pipe $4\frac{5}{7}$ gallons of water ran into a cistern in 1 minute; how much did the vessel hold, provided it was filled in 9 minutes?

56. If 7 men can perform a certain piece of work in $13\frac{1}{7}$ days; how long would it take 4 men to do the same?

57. If 5 persons consume a barrel of flour in 9 weeks, what part of a barrel would they consume in 5 weeks?

58. If a man earn $\frac{7}{8}$ in a day, and a boy $\frac{2}{3}$, how much will they both earn in 6 days?

59. Anthony spent $\frac{3}{4}$ of all his money, and the remainder he gave for 8 yards of cloth, at $2\frac{3}{4}$ a yard; how much had he at first?

60. From a piece of cloth a tailor cut 5 garments, each containing $3\frac{3}{7}$ yards, and there remained $2\frac{6}{7}$ yards; how many yards did the piece contain?

61. What will 9 pounds of rice cost, if 7 pounds cost 43 cents?

62. An individual, after spending $1\frac{3}{7}$ of all his money, had only $40 remaining; how much had he at first?

63. An old lady bought 30 eggs, at the rate of 2 for 5 cents; what did they cost?

64. How much will 13 pounds of coffee cost, if 26 pounds cost $7?

65. What will 7 gallons of molasses cost, if 6 pints cost 27 cents?

66. If 5 lamps cost $7\frac{1}{2}$, what will 7 lamps cost?

67. If 5 horses, in $4\frac{2}{5}$ days, consume 20 bushels of oats, in how many days can 11 horses consume the same?

68. If 15 gold pens cost $20, what will 5 of them cost?

69. If $\frac{1}{8}$ of an acre of land be worth $14, what are 10 acres worth?

70. $25 is $\frac{5}{9}$ of the cost of B's watch; what was the cost of his watch?

71. Mortimer's hat cost $5, and $\frac{2}{3}$ of the cost of his hat is $\frac{1}{12}$ of the cost of his coat; what was the cost of his coat?

72. If a man in $\frac{4}{15}$ of a day walk 8 miles, how far can he walk in 5 days?

73. From a piece of cloth containing 20 E. Fr., a tailor cut 8 suits of clothes, each containing $2\frac{3}{4}$ yards; how many yards remained?

74. If a man can cut 1 cord of wood in 5 hours; how many cords can he cut in 4 days, by working 12 hours a day?

75. A man bought 7 sheep, at the rate of 9 for $\$5\frac{1}{2}$, what did they cost him?

76. A boy bought 13 oranges,—giving 9 apples for 3 oranges; how many apples did his oranges cost him?

77. If 25 cents buy 7 lemons, how many cents will 9 lemons cost?

78. $\frac{3}{5}$ of 45 equals $\frac{3}{4}$ as many dollars as Andrew has; how many dollars has he?

79. $\$30\frac{5}{7}$ is $\frac{1}{7}$ of all the money A had; how much money had he?

80. What will 3 pecks of flax-seed cost, if 3 pints cost 3 dimes?

81. What will 1 quart of clover seed cost, if 5 pecks cost $3 and 2 dimes?

82. $4\frac{1}{2}$ times 7 is $\frac{1}{2}$ of what number?

83. $\frac{2}{6}$ of 36 is $\frac{4}{5}$ of what number?

84. $\frac{1}{3}$ of 36 is $1\frac{2}{5}$ times what number?

85. $\frac{2}{3}$ of A's age is 3 times B's age; and B is 9 years old. What is A's age?

86. An individual, being asked the number of hours he labored each day, answered, $1\frac{1}{8}$ times the number of hours in a day is 3 times as many hours as I labor. How many hours did he labor each day?

87. $\frac{3}{5}$ of 15 is $\frac{3}{7}$ of what number?

88. $\frac{4}{7}$ of 21 is $1\frac{1}{5}$ times what number?

89. $\frac{2}{3}$ of 24 is $1\frac{3}{5}$ times what number?

90. Wright is 16 years old, and $1\frac{3}{4}$ times his age is $1\frac{2}{5}$ times Charles' age. How old is Charles?

Lesson XII.

LESSONS EIGHTH, NINTH, AND TENTH COMBINED.

☞ REMARK.—*Pupils must exercise their own judgment in employing the shortest of the methods given in lessons eighth and tenth for multiplying and dividing.*

1. If 3 barrels of flour cost $\$13\frac{3}{4}$, what will 6 cost?

SOLUTION.—$$13\frac{3}{4}$ equals $$\frac{55}{4}$. If 3 barrels of flour cost $$\frac{55}{4}$, 6 barrels, which are 2 times 3 barrels, will cost 2 times $$\frac{55}{4}$ which are $$\frac{55}{2}$, or $$27\frac{1}{2}$.

2. If 5 pounds of opium cost $$27\frac{1}{2}$, what will 20 pounds cost?

3. If 3 pounds of sugar cost $17\frac{3}{8}$ cents, what will 24 pounds cost?

4. How many apples will pay for 9 oranges, if 8 apples are worth $12\frac{4}{5}$ oranges?

SOLUTION.—$12\frac{4}{5}$ oranges equal $\frac{64}{5}$ oranges. If $\frac{64}{5}$ oranges are worth 8 apples $\frac{1}{5}$ of an orange is worth $\frac{1}{64}$ of 8 apples, which is $\frac{8}{64}$, or $\frac{1}{8}$ of an apple, and $\frac{5}{5}$, which is 1 orange, are worth 5 times $\frac{1}{8}$, or $\frac{5}{8}$ of an apple, and 9 oranges are worth 9 times $\frac{5}{8}$, which are $\frac{45}{8}$, or $5\frac{5}{8}$ apples.

REMARK.—In solving questions in Proportion, never seek the value of a unit of the denomination like the answer.

5. How many chestnuts will pay for 9 walnuts, if 7 chestnuts are worth $10\frac{2}{7}$ walnuts?

6. If 8 barrels of flour cost $$33\frac{3}{5}$, what will 20 barrels cost?

7. If it require $9\frac{3}{8}$ yards of cloth to make 3 coats, how many yards will it require to make 8 coats?

8. If 10 men can perform a certain piece of work in $9\frac{3}{5}$ days, how long will it take 8 men to perform the same?

9. What will be the cost of 6 sheep, if 15 cost $$10\frac{1}{2}$?

10. If 1 person consume $10\frac{1}{26}$ bushels of wheat in a month, how much will 13 persons consume in the same time?

11. If $9\frac{7}{9}$ cents will buy 4 peaches, what will be the cost of 9 peaches?

12. If $$9\frac{1}{16}$ will pay for 5 weeks' board, how many dollars will pay for 8 weeks' board?

13. If 6 orifices will fill a vessel in $3\frac{3}{5}$ hours, how many of the same size will be required to fill it in $\frac{1}{15}$ of an hour?

14. If 9 men can build a boat in $5\frac{3}{4}$ days, in how many days could 6 men build it?

15. If 2 men in 4 days can earn $12, how many dollars can 7 men earn in the same time?

16. If I pay $17\frac{2}{3}$ cents for riding 4 miles, how much must I pay for riding 6 miles?

17. What will 1 year's board cost, at $5\frac{2}{3}$ for 4 weeks?

18. If 9 barrels of fish cost $54\frac{1}{3}$, what will 27 barrels cost?

19. How many dollars will 1 barrel of tobacco cost, if 17 barrels cost $51\frac{1}{2}$ eagles?

20. If 13 pounds of tea cost $10\frac{2}{5}$ dimes, what will 5 pounds cost?

21. If $7\frac{2}{3}$ tons of hay keep 6 horses through the winter, how many tons will keep 9 horses the same time?

22. A fox is 40 rods before a hound, and runs 3 rods to the hound's 5; how many rods must the hound run to overtake the fox? How far did the fox run?

23. How many dollars will a man earn in 14 days, if he earn $3\frac{2}{7}$ in 4 days?

24. A merchant bought 8 pieces of cloth, each piece containing 5 yards, for $32\frac{1}{2}$; how much did it cost a piece, and how much a yard?

25. If in a certain time 6 horses eat $14\frac{3}{4}$ bushels of oats, how many bushels will 8 horses eat in the same time?

26. A boy sold 3 lemons, at the rate of 6 for 8 cents; how much did he receive for them?

27. A boy gave $4\frac{1}{2}$ cents for oranges, at the rate of 5 oranges for $7\frac{1}{2}$ cents; how many did he buy?

28. If a piece of mahogany, weighing 9 pounds, is worth $2\frac{3}{4}$, what is the value of 12 pounds, at the same rate?

29. If a pole 8 feet long cast a shadow $4\frac{4}{5}$ feet, what will be the length of the shadow of a pole which is 15 feet long, at the same time of day?

30. At a certain time of day, a pole 5 feet long

casts a shadow $7\frac{1}{2}$ feet; what is the length of that pole which at the same time casts a shadow $4\frac{1}{2}$ feet?

31. If it require $\$21\frac{2}{5}$ worth of provisions to serve 8 men 2 days, how many dollars' worth will serve 5 men 4 days?

32. What is the length of a pole the shadow of which is 12 feet long, at the same time a pole $2\frac{2}{3}$ feet in length casts a shadow 4 feet long?

Lesson XIII.

REMARK.—By inspecting *Lessons* 8th and 10th, we observe, that, multiplying both *numerator* and *denominator* by the same number does not alter the value of a fraction. Hence, to convert a fraction to an equivalent fraction having a different denominator, we may multiply both numerator and denominator by any number which will cause the fraction to have the required denominator.

1. $\frac{3}{4}$ is how many eighths?

SOLUTION.—There are $\frac{4}{4}$ in one, and in $\frac{1}{4}$ there is $\frac{1}{4}$ of $\frac{4}{4}$, or $\frac{2}{8}$, and in $\frac{3}{4}$ there are 3 times $\frac{2}{8}$ or $\frac{6}{8}$.

REMARK.—Multiply each term of the given fraction by a number that will cause the denominator to become the required denominator. SOLUTION 2nd.—$\frac{3}{4}$ equal $\frac{6}{8}$.

2. $\frac{1}{4}$ is how many eighths?
3. $\frac{1}{5}$ is how many tenths
4. $\frac{1}{2}$ is how many sixths?
5. $\frac{1}{3}$ is how many sixths?
6. $\frac{1}{2}$ and $\frac{1}{3}$ are how many sixths?
7. $\frac{2}{3}$ are how many sixths?
8. $\frac{5}{6}$ are how many twelfths?
9. $\frac{2}{3}$ are how many twelfths
10. $\frac{3}{3}$ are how many eighteenths?
11. $\frac{3}{5}$ are how many tenths?
12. $\frac{2}{5}$ are how many tenths?
13. $\frac{4}{5}$ are how many twentieths?
14. $\frac{1}{2}$ is how many tenths?
15. Harris gave $\frac{2}{5}$ of an orange to his sister; how many fifteenths did he give her?

16. How many sixteenths in $\frac{3}{8}$?
17. How many sixteenths in $\frac{5}{8}$?
18. How many sixteenths in $\frac{7}{8}$?
19. How many fourteenths in $\frac{3}{7}$?
20. How many fourteenths in $\frac{5}{7}$?
21. How many fourteenths in $\frac{4}{7}$?
22. How many ninths in $\frac{2}{3}$?
23. How many twentieths in $\frac{4}{5}$?
24. How many fortieths in $\frac{7}{8}$?
25. How many forty-ninths in $\frac{5}{7}$?
26. How many fifteenths in $\frac{3}{5}$?

27. A man gave $\frac{1}{5}$ of a bushel of potatoes to one poor woman, and $\frac{3}{10}$ of a bushel to another; what part of a bushel did he give to both?

28. How could you divide an apple so as to give $\frac{2}{3}$ of it to 1 boy, and $\frac{1}{4}$ of it to another?

29. $\frac{2}{5} + \frac{2}{3}$ are how many fifteenths?

SOLUTION.—$\frac{2}{5}$ equals $\frac{6}{15}$, and $\frac{2}{3}$ equals $\frac{10}{15}$, $\frac{6}{15}$ and $\frac{10}{15}$ are $\frac{16}{15}$, or $1 \frac{1}{15}$.

30. $\frac{3}{4} + \frac{2}{3}$ are how many twelfths?
31. $\frac{5}{9} + \frac{1}{2}$ are how many eighteenths?
32. $\frac{7}{8} + \frac{2}{3}$ are how many twenty-fourths?
33. $\frac{3}{7}$ are how many times $\frac{3}{21}$?
34. What is the sum of $\frac{3}{4}$ and $\frac{3}{8}$?
35. What is the sum of $\frac{3}{7}$ and $\frac{2}{5}$?
36. What is the sum of $\frac{1}{3}$ and $\frac{3}{7}$?
37. What is the sum of $\frac{2}{3}$ and $\frac{3}{5}$?
38. What is the sum of $\frac{3}{4}$ and $\frac{7}{8}$?
39. What is the sum of $\frac{1}{2}$ and $\frac{2}{3}$?
40. What is the sum of $\frac{5}{9}$ and $\frac{2}{3}$?
41. What is the sum of $\frac{7}{9}$ and $\frac{1}{2}$?
42. What is the sum of $\frac{4}{5}$ and $\frac{4}{7}$?
43. What is the sum of $\frac{5}{6}$, $\frac{1}{2}$ and $\frac{2}{3}$?
44. What is the sum of $\frac{3}{4}$, $\frac{2}{3}$ and $\frac{5}{8}$?
45. From $\frac{3}{4}$ subtract $\frac{1}{2}$.
46. From $\frac{5}{6}$ subtract $\frac{2}{3}$.
47. From $\frac{5}{7}$ subtract $\frac{1}{3}$.

48. From $2\frac{1}{3}$ subtract $\frac{3}{7}$.
49. From 4 subtract $\frac{1}{2}$.
50. From 3 subtract $\frac{3}{5}$.
51. From 9 subtract $\frac{3}{4}$.
52. From 5 subtract $\frac{4}{5}$.
53. From 3 subtract $1\frac{1}{2}$.
54. From 9 subtract $2\frac{2}{3}$.
55. From 6 subtract $3\frac{3}{4}$.
56. $14-3\frac{1}{2}$ are how many？
57. $7-2\frac{5}{6}$ are how many？
58. $9-3\frac{4}{7}$ are how many？
59. $10-3\frac{5}{8}$ are how many？
60. $12-3\frac{4}{9}$ are how many？
61. $13-7\frac{2}{11}$ are how many？
62. $9\frac{2}{3}-4\frac{1}{2}$ are how many？
63. $7\frac{2}{4}-5\frac{3}{7}$ are how many？
64. $3\frac{1}{2}-1\frac{4}{5}$ are how many？
65. $4\frac{3}{7}-1\frac{5}{8}$ are how many？
66. $5\frac{3}{5}-2\frac{2}{3}$ are how many？
67. $9\frac{3}{5}-7\frac{2}{3}$ are how many？
68. $2\frac{3}{4}+3\frac{1}{4}-\frac{3}{5}$ are how many？
69. $4\frac{2}{3}+5\frac{3}{4}-2\frac{3}{5}$ are how many？
70. $3\frac{5}{6}+4\frac{1}{6}-\frac{7}{8}$ are how many？
71. $9\frac{2}{3}+3\frac{3}{4}-3$ are how many？
72. $\frac{2}{3}+\frac{3}{4}-\frac{7}{8}$ are how many？
73. $\frac{5}{6}+\frac{1}{3}+\frac{5}{7}-\frac{1}{2}$ are how many？
74. $2\frac{1}{8}$ are how many times $\frac{2}{16}$？
75. $3\frac{1}{3}$ are how many times $\frac{4}{10}$？
76. $\frac{9}{13}$ are how many times $\frac{3}{26}$？
77. $\frac{1}{2}$ are how many times $\frac{6}{36}$？
78. $\frac{4}{7}$ are how many times $\frac{2}{14}$？
79. $1\frac{1}{8}$ are how many times $\frac{3}{16}$？
80. $\frac{7}{9}$ are how many times $\frac{2}{18}$？
81. $\frac{5}{13}$ are how many times $\frac{5}{26}$？
82. $8\frac{2}{3}$ are how many times $2\frac{1}{6}$？
83. $10\frac{4}{5}$ are how many times $\frac{9}{15}$？
84. $12\frac{1}{2}$ are how many times $1\frac{1}{4}$？

85. $\frac{1}{6}+\frac{1}{5}+\frac{1}{4}$ is how much less than a whole one?

86. $\frac{1}{7}+\frac{2}{6}+\frac{2}{5}$ is how much less than a whole one

87. A lady gave $\frac{1}{2}$ of all her money for a dress, and $\frac{3}{4}$ of it for a shawl; what part of her money had she remaining?

88. $\frac{1}{2}$ of an army was killed, and $\frac{1}{3}$ taken prisoners; what part of the army escaped?

89. $\frac{3}{8}$ of an army was killed, $\frac{5}{6}$ taken prisoners, and 500 escaped; how many were there in the army?

90. $\frac{2}{3}$ of the length of a pole is in the ground, $\frac{1}{5}$ of it in the water, and 12 feet in the air; what is the length of the pole?

91. A market woman sold $\frac{5}{9}$ of all her oranges to one man and $\frac{1}{4}$ of them to another, and then had only 9 remaining; how many had she at first, and how many did she sell to each?

92. A man, after spending $\frac{3}{4}$ of his fortune, found that $20 was $\frac{2}{9}$ of what he had remaining; what was his fortune?

93. A hawk caught $\frac{2}{5}$ of Euphemia's chickens, a cat killed $\frac{1}{3}$ of them, $\frac{1}{7}$ of them died, and she had 13 remaining; how many had she at first, and how many were destroyed by the hawk and cat respectively?

94. Said A to B, if to my age you add its and $\frac{1}{2}$ its $\frac{2}{5}$, the sum will be 38; how old was he?

95. A is 40 years old, and $\frac{3}{4}$ of his age is $\frac{3}{5}$ of twice as much as his wife's age; how old was his wife?

Lesson IV.

REMARK.—By inspecting *Lessons* 8th and 10th, we observe that dividing both *numerator* and *denominator* of a fraction by the same number does not alter its value. Hence, to reduce a fraction to its lowest terms, we may divide both numerator and denominator by any number that is contained in each of them without a remainder.

1 Reduce $\frac{4}{8}$ to its lowest terms.

2. Reduce $\frac{3}{9}$ to its lowest terms.

3. Reduce $\frac{3}{6}$ to its lowest terms.

4. Reduce $\frac{5}{15}$ to its lowest terms.

5. Reduce $\frac{4}{12}$ to its lowest terms.

6. Reduce $\frac{12}{24}$ to its lowest terms.

7. Reduce $\frac{15}{25}$ to its lowest terms.

8. Reduce $\frac{35}{75}$ to its lowest terms.

9. Reduce $\frac{36}{48}$ to its lowest terms.

10. Reduce $\frac{25}{35}$ to its lowest terms.

11. Reduce $\frac{36}{60}$ to its lowest terms.

12. Reduce $\frac{75}{100}$ to its lowest terms.

13. Reduce $\frac{32}{56}$ to its lowest terms.

14. Reduce $\frac{50}{70}$ to its lowest terms.

15. Reduce $\frac{12}{18}$ to its lowest terms.

16. Why does the value of the fraction remain the same, when you divide both *numerator* and *denominator* by the same number?

17. When you multiply both numerator and denominator by the same number, why does it not change the value of the fraction?

18. Reduce 4 times $\frac{6}{12}$ to its lowest terms.

19. Reduce 7 times $\frac{4}{14}$ to its lowest terms.

20. Reduce 8 times $2\frac{1}{4}$ to its lowest terms.

21. Reduce 6 times $\frac{5}{24}$ to its lowest terms.

22. Reduce 4 times $\frac{5}{15}$ to its lowest terms.

23. Reduce 12 times $\frac{3}{18}$ to its lowest terms.

24. Reduce 12 times $\frac{5}{48}$ to its lowest terms.

25. Reduce 8 times $\frac{2}{24}$ to its lowest terms.

26. Reduce 7 times $\frac{3}{35}$ to its lowest terms.

27. Reduce 5 times $1\frac{4}{35}$ to its lowest terms.

28. Reduce 4 times $\frac{3}{36}$ to its lowest terms.

29. Reduce 6 times $\frac{18}{36}$ to its lowest terms.

30. Reduce 9 times $\frac{27}{81}$ to its lowest terms.

Lesson XV.

1. If you cut an apple into two equal pieces, what will 1 of these pieces be called?

2. If you cut $\frac{1}{2}$ an apple into two equal pieces, what part of a whole apple will 1 of these pieces bo called?

3. If Alice has $\frac{1}{3}$ of a lemon, and gives half of it to Ann, what part of a lemon will Ann receive?

SOLUTION.—$\frac{1}{3}$ equals $\frac{2}{6}$. Therefore Ann receives $\frac{1}{2}$ of $\frac{2}{6}$ of a lemon, which is $\frac{1}{6}$ of a lemon.

4. George, having half of a melon, gave $\frac{1}{2}$ of it to Marcus; what part of a melon did Marcus receive?

5. Crary had $\frac{1}{4}$ of a dollar, and gave $\frac{1}{2}$ of it to Joshua; what part of a dollar did Joshua receive?

6. Robert had $\frac{1}{5}$ of a dollar, and gave $\frac{1}{2}$ of it for a cake; how many cents did the cake cost him?

7. Margaret had $\frac{1}{6}$ of a pound of candies, and Mary had $\frac{1}{2}$ as much; how much had Mary?

8. Jane had $\frac{1}{5}$ of a pound of sugar, and Ann $\frac{1}{4}$ as much; how much had Ann?

9. A boy bought $\frac{1}{5}$ of a quart of chestnuts, and gave $\frac{1}{3}$ of them to his sister; what part of a quart did she receive?

10. A man owned $\frac{1}{9}$ of a share in a bank, and sold $\frac{1}{2}$ of that; what part of a share had he remaining?

11. B owned $\frac{1}{6}$ of a ship, and sold $\frac{1}{4}$ of his share; what part part of a whole ship did he sell?

12. What is $\frac{1}{3}$ of $\frac{1}{5}$?

SOLUTION.—$\frac{1}{3}$ of $\frac{1}{5}$ is $\frac{1}{15}$.

13.	What	is	$\frac{1}{5}$	of	$\frac{1}{2}$?
14.	What	is	$\frac{1}{3}$	of	$\frac{1}{7}$?
15.	What	is	$\frac{1}{4}$	of	$\frac{1}{6}$?
16.	What	is	$\frac{1}{8}$	of	$\frac{1}{9}$?
17.	What	is	$\frac{1}{4}$	of	$\frac{1}{9}$?
18.	What	is	$\frac{1}{7}$	of	$\frac{1}{4}$?

19   What   is $\frac{1}{2}$ of $1\frac{1}{5}$?
20.   What   is $\frac{1}{11}$ of $1\frac{1}{2}$?

21. A kite was up in the air and fell $\frac{7}{8}$ of the way to the ground, it then arose $\frac{1}{9}$ of its distance from the ground; what part of the whole distance was it above the ground?

22. Homer is $\frac{1}{5}$ as old as his father, and Nelson is $\frac{1}{4}$ as old as Homer; what part of the father's age is Nelson's age?

23. A man, owning $\frac{1}{7}$ of a barrel of fish, accommodated his neighbor with $\frac{1}{7}$ of it; how much had he remaining?

24. A man, having $\frac{1}{2}$ of an eagle, gave $\frac{1}{5}$ of it to B, and B gave $\frac{1}{10}$ of what he had to C; what part of an eagle had each after this division, and how many cents had each?

25. Elizabeth had $\frac{2}{3}$ of a pie, and gave $\frac{1}{3}$ of it to Harriet; how much did she receive?

SOLUTION.—$\frac{1}{3}$ of $\frac{1}{3}$ is $\frac{1}{9}$; and if $\frac{1}{3}$ of $\frac{1}{3}$ is $\frac{1}{9}$, $\frac{1}{3}$ of $\frac{2}{3}$ is twice $\frac{1}{9}$, which are $\frac{2}{9}$. Therefore Harriet had $\frac{2}{9}$ of a pie.

Or, SOLUTION.—$\frac{1}{3}$ of $\frac{2}{3}$ is $\frac{2}{9}$.

26.   What   is $\frac{1}{2}$ of $\frac{3}{5}$?
27.   What   is $\frac{1}{4}$ of $\frac{2}{3}$?
28.   What   is $\frac{1}{5}$ of $\frac{2}{3}$?
29.   What   is $\frac{1}{6}$ of $\frac{3}{4}$?
30.   What   is $\frac{1}{7}$ of $\frac{1}{4}$?
31.   What   is $\frac{1}{8}$ of $\frac{3}{4}$?
32.   What   is $\frac{1}{9}$ of $\frac{2}{3}$?
33.   What   is $\frac{1}{9}$ of $\frac{4}{5}$?
34.   What   is $\frac{1}{8}$ of $\frac{5}{7}$?
35.   What   is $\frac{1}{5}$ of $\frac{3}{4}$?
36.   What   is $\frac{1}{1}$ of   ?
37.   What   is $\frac{1}{9}$ of $\frac{5}{7}$?
38.   What   is $\frac{1}{7}$ of $\frac{5}{7}$?
39.   What   is $\frac{1}{7}$ of $1\frac{5}{7}$?
40.   What   is $\frac{2}{3}$ of $\frac{4}{}$?

7

41. What is $\frac{3}{4}$ of $\frac{1}{5}$?
42. What is $\frac{3}{4}$ of $\frac{1}{7}$?
43. What is $\frac{3}{5}$ of $\frac{1}{9}$?
44. What is $\frac{5}{6}$ of $\frac{1}{7}$?
45. What is $\frac{3}{7}$ of $\frac{1}{5}$?
46. What is $\frac{3}{8}$ of $\frac{1}{9}$?
47. What is $\frac{7}{8}$ of $\frac{1}{4}$?
48. What is $\frac{5}{7}$ of $\frac{1}{8}$?
49. What is $\frac{4}{5}$ of $\frac{1}{6}$?
50. What is $\frac{3}{7}$ of $\frac{1}{4}$?
51. What is $\frac{2}{3}$ of $\frac{3}{5}$?
52. What is $\frac{3}{4}$ of $\frac{4}{5}$?
53. What is $\frac{3}{5}$ of $\frac{2}{7}$?
54. What is $\frac{3}{4}$ of $\frac{2}{3}$?
55. What is $\frac{4}{5}$ of $\frac{3}{8}$?
56. What is $\frac{3}{8}$ of $\frac{5}{7}$?
57. What is $\frac{3}{5}$ of $\frac{6}{7}$?
58. What is $\frac{4}{7}$ of $\frac{8}{9}$?
59. What is $\frac{5}{7}$ of $\frac{6}{7}$?
60. What is $\frac{8}{13}$ of $\frac{2}{3}$?
61. What part of 1 is $\frac{3}{7}$ of $\frac{1}{1}$?
62. What part of 2 is $\frac{4}{6}$ of $\frac{1}{3}$?

SOLUTION.—$\frac{4}{6}$ of $\frac{1}{3}$ is $\frac{2}{9}$. $\frac{2}{9}$ is $\frac{2}{9}$ of 1, and is therefore $\frac{1}{9}$ of 2, which is $\frac{1}{9}$ of 2.

SOLUTION 2nd.—$\frac{4}{6}$ of $\frac{1}{3}$ is $\frac{2}{9}$. 1 is $\frac{1}{2}$ of 2. If 1 is $\frac{1}{2}$ of 2, $\frac{1}{9}$ is $\frac{1}{2}$ of $\frac{1}{9}$, or $\frac{1}{18}$ of 2, and $\frac{2}{9}$ are 2 times $\frac{1}{18}$, or $\frac{1}{9}$ of 2.

64. What part of 2 is $\frac{1}{4}$ of $1\frac{4}{5}$?
65. What part of 2 is $\frac{3}{4}$ of $\frac{1}{3}$?
66. What part of 3 is $\frac{1}{2}$ of $\frac{1}{2}$?
67. What part of 4 is $\frac{1}{3}$ of $1\frac{4}{5}$?
68. What part of 5 is $\frac{1}{6}$ of $\frac{2}{3}$?
69. What part of 9 is $\frac{3}{4}$ of $1\frac{1}{3}$?
70. What part of 2 is $\frac{2}{3}$ of $\frac{4}{5}$?
71. What part of 2 is $\frac{3}{4}$ of $2\frac{1}{2}$?
72. What part of 4 is $\frac{5}{6}$ of $\frac{8}{10}$?
73. What part of 6 is $\frac{7}{9}$ of $\frac{6}{8}$?
74. What part of 3 is $\frac{1}{2}$ of $4\frac{1}{5}$?

75. What part of 4 is $\frac{5}{6}$ of $12\frac{5}{6}$?

76. What part of 7 is $\frac{2}{3}$ of $10\frac{3}{4}$?

77. Anthony had $\frac{1}{3}$ of $\frac{3}{4}$ of a pound of cinnamon; what part of a pound had he?

78. Albert had $\frac{1}{7}$ of $\frac{2}{3}$ of a quart of strawberries; how many strawberries had he, provided 1 quart contained 42 strawberries?

79. Abner gave $\frac{1}{2}$ of $\frac{6}{7}$ of a melon to his brother; what part of a melon had he remaining?

80. Matilda bought $\frac{5}{6}$ of a quart of milk for tea, and spilled $\frac{1}{3}$ of it; what part of a quart had she remaining?

81. Edwin picked $\frac{7}{8}$ of a pailful of blackberries, and on his way home spilled $\frac{1}{3}$ of them; what part of a pailful had he remaining?

82. A merchant bought $\frac{4}{5}$ of a hogshead of molasses, and $\frac{1}{3}$ of it leaked out; what part of a hogshead had he remaining?

83. Mirriam had $\frac{2}{3}$ of a pound of candies, and gave $\frac{3}{4}$ of them to Augusta; what part of a pound did she give Augusta?

84. Elisha found $\$\frac{3}{4}$ and gave $\frac{2}{5}$ of it to Ephraim; what part of a dollar had he remaining?

85. Andrew bought $\frac{4}{5}$ of a pound of maple sugar, and gave $\frac{2}{3}$ of it to Walter; what part of a pound did Walter receive?

86. Jacob, having a pine-apple, gave $\frac{2}{3}$ of $\frac{4}{5}$ of it to the one who could tell how much that would be; what part of a pine-apple had Jacob remaining?

87. James gave $\frac{2}{3}$ of $\frac{3}{5}$ of a dime for a top; how many cents did the top cost him?

88. Robert gave $\frac{3}{4}$ of a dollar for a cap; how many cents did the cap cost him?

89. Mary gave $\frac{7}{8}$ of $1\frac{3}{5}$ dimes for a comb; how many cents did the comb cost her?

90. Clarinda gave $\frac{2}{3}$ of 6 dimes for a pair of gloves; how many cents did the gloves cost her?

91. A man, having $4\frac{3}{5}$ barrels of flour, sold $\frac{1}{3}$ of it; how much remained unsold?

92. A man gave $\frac{2}{3}$ of $3\frac{1}{2}$ for a silver pencil; what was the cost of the pencil?

93. Jane worked $8\frac{3}{4}$ hours in a day, and Delilah worked only $\frac{4}{5}$ as many; how many hours did Delilah work in a day?

94. B gave $32\frac{2}{3}$ for a cow, which was $\frac{2}{3}$ as much as A gave for his; how much more did A's cow cost than B's?

95. Darius is $18\frac{3}{4}$ years old, which was $\frac{3}{4}$ of Daniel's age; how old is he?

96. If 1 yard of cloth cost $5\frac{3}{4}$, what will $\frac{2}{3}$ of a yard cost?

97. If 4 yards of cloth cost $9\frac{1}{2}$, what will $\frac{4}{5}$ of a yard cost?

98. If 5 barrels of beef cost $18\frac{1}{3}$, what will $\frac{1}{2}$ of a barrel cost?

99. If $\frac{2}{3}$ of an apple cost $\frac{3}{4}$ of a cent, what will 1 apple cost?

100. If $\frac{1}{4}$ of an orange cost $1\frac{1}{3}$ cents, what will $\frac{5}{16}$ of an orange cost?

101. If 4 pounds of butter cost $6\frac{1}{4}$ dimes, how many cents will $1\frac{3}{5}$ pounds cost?

Lesson XVI.

1. If 4 bls. of flour cost $14\frac{2}{3}$, what will $\frac{5}{6}$ of a bl. cost?

2. If 3 bush. of pears cost $5\frac{1}{7}$, what will $1\frac{1}{6}$ bush. cost?

3. If $2\frac{1}{2}$ bushels of apples cost $6\frac{1}{4}$ dimes, how many cents will $\frac{4}{5}$ of a bushel cost?

4. If $\frac{3}{4}$ of an apple cost $\frac{2}{3}$ of a cent, what will 1 apple cost?

5. If $\frac{3}{8}$ of an orange cost $\frac{3}{4}$ of a cent, what will $\frac{3}{4}$ of an orange cost?

6. If $2\frac{3}{4}$ yds. of silk cost $3\frac{5}{8}$, what will $5\frac{1}{2}$ yds. cost?

7. If $5\frac{2}{5}$ yds. of satin cost $5\frac{4}{10}$, what will 2 yds cost?

8. If in $3\frac{4}{7}$ hours A can do a piece of work, how long will it take him to do a piece $1\frac{2}{5}$ times as large?

9. $\frac{3}{4}$ of A's age is $\frac{2}{3}$ of B's age; and $\frac{3}{4}$ of B's age is $\frac{2}{3}$ of C's age. How old are A and B respectively, provided C is 81 years old?

10. Bought $3\frac{2}{3}$ boxes of goods, at $6\frac{6}{11}$ a box, and paid for them with sheep at $2 a head; how many sheep did it take?

11. How many times $\frac{2}{5}$ is $\frac{3}{4}$?

SOLUTION 1ST.—$\frac{2}{5}$ equals $\frac{8}{20}$, and $\frac{3}{4}$ equals $\frac{15}{20}$. $\frac{8}{20}$ is contained in $\frac{15}{20}$, $\frac{15}{8}$ or $1\frac{7}{8}$ times.

SOLUTION 2ND.—$\frac{2}{5}$ is contained in 1, $\frac{5}{2}$ times, and in $\frac{3}{4}$, $\frac{3}{4}$ times $\frac{5}{2}$ times, which are $\frac{15}{8}$, or $1\frac{7}{8}$ times.

SOLUTION 3RD.—1 is contained in $\frac{3}{4}$, $\frac{3}{4}$ times. If 1 is contained in $\frac{3}{4}$, $\frac{3}{4}$ times, $\frac{1}{5}$ is contained in $\frac{3}{4}$ 5 times $\frac{3}{4}$ times, which are $\frac{15}{4}$ times, and $\frac{2}{5}$ is contained in it, $\frac{1}{2}$ of $\frac{15}{4}$ times, which is $\frac{15}{8}$, or $1\frac{7}{8}$ times.

12.	How	many	times	$\frac{2}{3}$	is	$\frac{3}{4}$?
13.	How	many ·	times	$\frac{2}{3}$	is	$\frac{7}{8}$?
14.	How	many	times	$\frac{3}{5}$	is	$\frac{6}{7}$?
15.	How	many	times	$\frac{3}{8}$	is	$\frac{3}{16}$?
16.	How	many	times	$\frac{2}{3}$	is	$1\frac{1}{8}$?
17.	How	many	times	$\frac{2}{7}$	is	$\frac{4}{14}$?
18.	How	many	times	$\frac{2}{5}$	is	$\frac{7}{4}$?
19.	How	many	times	$\frac{4}{5}$	is	$3\frac{3}{7}$?
20.	How	many	times	$\frac{3}{4}$	is	$2\frac{2}{3}$?
21.	How	many	times	$\frac{3}{7}$	is	$2\frac{2}{5}$?
22.	How	many	times	$\frac{5}{9}$	is	$5\frac{5}{6}$?
23.	How	many	times	$\frac{2}{5}$	is	$\frac{3}{10}$?
24.	How	many	times	$\frac{4}{7}$	is	$\frac{12}{14}$?
25.	How	many	times	$\frac{5}{8}$	is	$3\frac{1}{9}$?
26.	How	many	times	$\frac{7}{8}$	is	$4\frac{1}{3}$?
27.	How	many	times	$1\frac{1}{2}$	is	$2\frac{1}{2}$?

28. How many times $2\frac{2}{3}$ is $1\frac{3}{5}$?
29. How many times $3\frac{1}{4}$ is $5\frac{1}{6}$?
30. How many times $4\frac{2}{3}$ is $5\frac{3}{5}$?

31. A farmer sold a quantity of rye for \$96, which was only $\frac{4}{5}$ of what it was worth; how much did he lose by the bargain?

32. A man sold a cow for $1\frac{3}{8}$ times what she cost him, and by so doing gained \$6; how much did the cow cost him?

33. A merchant sold a quantity of goods for $\frac{13}{18}$ of what they cost, and by so doing he lost \$15; how much did the goods cost him?

34. A farmer, having lost 12 sheep, found that only $\frac{7}{9}$ of his flock remained; how many sheep had he remaining?

35. An individual being asked how many geese he had, answered, that if to $\frac{5}{7}$ of the flock 24 geese were added, the sum would equal $1\frac{2}{7}$ times his original flock; how many geese had he?

36. If $\frac{2}{3}$ of a yard of cloth cost \$$\frac{3}{4}$, what will $\frac{2}{5}$ of a yard cost?

37. A boy, being asked his age, said, that $8\frac{1}{4}$ years was $\frac{3}{8}$ of twice as much as his age; how old was he?

38. If $\frac{3}{5}$ of the candies I have cost $7\frac{1}{2}$ cents, what will $\frac{7}{8}$ of them cost?

39. What will $\frac{5}{6}$ of a barrel of flour cost, if $\frac{4}{7}$ of a barrel cost $\$2\frac{1}{7}$?

40. What will $\frac{2}{3}$ of an orange cost, if $\frac{4}{7}$ of an orange cost $2\frac{1}{7}$ cents?

41. How many yards of cloth will be required to make a coat, if $1\frac{2}{3}$ will make $\frac{2}{8}$ of a coat?

42. $\frac{3}{4}$ of 2 are how many times $\frac{2}{3}$?
43. $\frac{3}{16}$ of 8 are how many times $\frac{1}{4}$?
44. $\frac{3}{5}$ of 7 are how many times 3?
45. $\frac{3}{4}$ of 8 are how many times $\frac{3}{6}$?
46. $\frac{3}{4}$ of 12 are how many times $\frac{2}{5}$ of 6?

47. $\frac{2}{5}$ of 7 are how many times $\frac{3}{5}$ of 2?

48. If $\frac{2}{5}$ of 3 yards of cloth cost $1\frac{1}{5}$, what will $\frac{3}{5}$ of 7 yards cost?

49. If $\frac{2}{7}$ of 6 yards of cloth cost $2\frac{3}{7}$, how much will $\frac{3}{5}$ of 7 yards cost?

50. If $\frac{2}{3}$ of $\frac{3}{4}$ of a barrel of flour cost $1\frac{2}{3}$, what will $\frac{1}{2}$ of $\frac{2}{3}$ of $\frac{3}{4}$ of a barrel cost?

Lesson XVII.

1. 12 is $\frac{3}{4}$ of what number?

Solution.—If $\frac{3}{4}$ of some number is 12, $\frac{1}{4}$ of that number is $\frac{1}{3}$ of 12, or 4; and $\frac{4}{4}$, which is that number, are 4 times 4, which are 16. Therefore 12 is $\frac{3}{4}$ of 16.

2.	15	is	$\frac{3}{5}$	of	what	number?
3.	18	is	$\frac{2}{7}$	of	what	number?
4.	20	is	$\frac{4}{5}$	of	what	number?
5.	26	is	$\frac{2}{3}$	of	what	number?
6.	25	is	$\frac{5}{7}$	of	what	number?
7.	30	is	$\frac{5}{6}$	of	what	number?
8.	32	is	$\frac{8}{9}$	of	what	number?
9.	39	is	$\frac{6}{7}$	of	what	number?
10.	36	is	$\frac{6}{11}$	of	what	number?
11.	36	is	$\frac{9}{5}$	of	what	number?
12.	24	is	$\frac{6}{7}$	of	what	number?
13.	9	is	$\frac{3}{7}$	of	what	number?
14.	12	is	$\frac{4}{5}$	of	what	number?
15.	38	is	$\frac{2}{3}$	of	what	number?
16.	16	is	$\frac{4}{5}$	of	what	number?
17.	16	is	$\frac{4}{7}$	of	what	number?
18.	16	is	$\frac{2}{5}$	of	what	number?
19.	40	is	$\frac{5}{8}$	of	what	number?
20.	40	is	$\frac{8}{9}$	of	what	number?

Solution.—40 is $\frac{8}{9}$ of 45.

Remark.—When pupils are familiar with the analysis of these questions, the intermediate steps may be omitted, as in the above solution.

21. 72 is $\frac{8}{9}$ of what number?
22. 72 is $\frac{9}{10}$ of what number?
23. 12 is $\frac{2}{3}$ of how many times 2?
24. 16 is $\frac{4}{9}$ of how many times 3?
25. 18 is $\frac{2}{5}$ of how many times 9?
26. 32 is $\frac{4}{7}$ of how many times 4?
27. 46 is $\frac{2}{3}$ of how many times 23?
28. 48 is $\frac{4}{5}$ of how many times 5?
29. 48 is $\frac{4}{7}$ of how many times 4?
30. 36 is $\frac{6}{7}$ of how many times 2?
31. 30 is $\frac{5}{6}$ of how many times $\frac{1}{2}$ of 12?
32. 30 is $\frac{6}{7}$ of how many times $\frac{1}{2}$ of 10?
33. 16 is $\frac{4}{9}$ of how many times $\frac{2}{3}$ of 9?
34. 16 is $\frac{4}{13}$ of how many times $\frac{3}{4}$ of 16?
35. 24 is $\frac{3}{8}$ of how many times $\frac{2}{3}$ of 12?
36. 25 is $\frac{5}{9}$ of how many times $\frac{1}{3}$ of 9?
37. 35 is $\frac{5}{12}$ of how many times $\frac{2}{3}$ of 9?
38. 40 is $\frac{5}{8}$ of how many times $\frac{4}{5}$ of 10?
39. 48 is $\frac{6}{10}$ of how many times $\frac{4}{5}$ of 25?
40. 96 is $\frac{2}{3}$ of how many times $\frac{3}{4}$ of 16?

Lesson XVIII.

1. $\frac{2}{3}$ of 6 is $\frac{2}{3}$ of what number?
2. $\frac{5}{6}$ of 10 is $\frac{2}{3}$ of what number?
3. $\frac{3}{4}$ of 8 is $\frac{2}{7}$ of what number?
4. $\frac{2}{7}$ of 21 is $\frac{4}{5}$ of what number?
5. $\frac{4}{5}$ of 15 is $\frac{3}{10}$ of what number?
6. $\frac{3}{10}$ of 40 is $\frac{4}{5}$ of what number?
7. $\frac{3}{4}$ of 27 is $\frac{3}{5}$ of what number?
8. $\frac{5}{6}$ of 27 is $\frac{8}{13}$ of what number?
9. $\frac{5}{9}$ of 81 is $\frac{9}{10}$ of what number?
10. $\frac{6}{7}$ of 49 is $\frac{6}{7}$ of what number?
11. $\frac{2}{3}$ of 12 is   of how many times 2?
12. $\frac{3}{4}$ of 16 is   of how many times 2?
13. $\frac{4}{5}$ of 10 is   of how many times 4?

14. $\frac{1}{4}$ of 16 is $\frac{2}{15}$ of how many times 6?
15. $\frac{4}{5}$ of 15 is $\frac{2}{7}$ of how many times 6?
16. $\frac{2}{5}$ of 20 is $\frac{2}{3}$ of how many times 3?
17. $\frac{5}{6}$ of 12 is $\frac{2}{9}$ of how many times 5?
18. $\frac{3}{4}$ of 20 is $\frac{4}{9}$ of how many times 3?
19. $\frac{7}{8}$ of 36 is $2\frac{1}{10}$ of how many times 4?
20. $\frac{8}{9}$ of 72 is $\frac{2}{3}$ of how many times 12?

SOLUTION.—$\frac{8}{9}$ of 72 is 64. 64 is $\frac{2}{3}$ of 96. 96 is 8 times 12.

21. $\frac{9}{8}$ of 96 is $\frac{2}{5}$ of how many times 90?
22. $\frac{7}{9}$ of 117 is $\frac{7}{8}$ of how many times 4?
23. $\frac{5}{7}$ of 56 is $\frac{5}{6}$ of how many times 8?
24. $\frac{5}{6}$ of 60 is $\frac{2}{3}$ of how many times 5?
25. $\frac{2}{3}$ of 36 is $\frac{2}{5}$ of how many times 12?
26. $\frac{3}{4}$ of 72 is $\frac{9}{8}$ of how many times 5?
27. $\frac{7}{8}$ of 40 is $\frac{5}{12}$ of how many times 21?
28. $\frac{5}{8}$ of 32 is $\frac{4}{9}$ of how many times 9?
29. $\frac{2}{3}$ of 15 is $\frac{5}{7}$ of how many times 2?
30. $\frac{3}{5}$ of 15 is $\frac{1}{3}$ of how many times 9?
31. $\frac{5}{6}$ of 24 is $\frac{5}{4}$ of how many times 3?
32. $\frac{7}{9}$ of 45 is $\frac{5}{6}$ of how many times 3?
33. $\frac{5}{7}$ of 14 is $\frac{2}{9}$ of how many times 5?
34. $\frac{7}{9}$ of 18 is $\frac{2}{9}$ of how many times 7?
35. $\frac{9}{10}$ of 40 is $\frac{3}{8}$ of how many times 6?
36. $\frac{4}{5}$ of 45 is $\frac{6}{11}$ of how many times 3?
37. $\frac{6}{7}$ of 35 is $\frac{5}{9}$ of how many times 2?
38. $\frac{8}{9}$ of 81 is $\frac{4}{5}$ of how many times 9?
39. $\frac{2}{3}$ of 5 is $\frac{5}{7}$ of how many times 7?
40. $\frac{3}{4}$ of 7 is $\frac{3}{5}$ of how many times 3?

41. B's horse cost $60, and $\frac{4}{5}$ of the cost of the horse is $\frac{1}{4}$ of two times the value of his wagon; what is the value of his wagon?

42. A coat cost $20, and $\frac{4}{5}$ of the cost of the coat is $\frac{2}{7}$ of 8 times the price of a hat; the price of the hat is required?

43. If a cow cost $30, and $\frac{2}{3}$ of this is $\frac{2}{7}$ of 10 times the price of a sheep, what is the price of a sheep?

44. A's farm is worth $1200, and $\frac{4}{5}$ of its value is $\frac{3}{4}$ of 10 times the value of its yearly productions; what is the value of the yearly productions?

45. The articles contained in a certain store cost $500, and $\frac{3}{10}$ of their cost is $\frac{2}{5}$ of 3 times the amount paid for the silks; how much was the cost of the silks, and of the other articles respectively?

46. A's wedding clothes cost $180, and $\frac{2}{3}$ of the cost of his clothes is $\frac{2}{9}$ of 6 times the cost of his wife's wedding dress; how much was the cost of her dress?

47. The insurance of a ship amounted to $800, and $\frac{1}{4}$ of that is $\frac{1}{20}$ of 2 times the value of the cargo; what is the value of the cargo?

48. A's house cost $1400, and $\frac{7}{4}$ of its cost is $3\frac{1}{3}$ times $\frac{1}{2}$ of the cost of the furniture contained in it; what was the cost of the furniture?

49. Provided a house was worth $1200, and $\frac{3}{4}$ of its value was $\frac{2}{3}$ of $\frac{1}{4}$ times the value of the farm on which it stood, what was the value of the farm?

50. If a sleigh cost $100, what would be the cost of a wagon, if $\frac{2}{5}$ of the cost of the sleigh was $\frac{2}{11}$ of twice the cost of a wagon?

51. Lambert is worth $2500, and $\frac{4}{5}$ of his fortune is $3\frac{1}{3}$ times $\frac{1}{2}$ of Latham's fortune; how much is Latham worth?

Distances on the Railroad between Albany and Buffalo.

52. The distance from Albany to Schenectady is 16 miles, and $\frac{3}{4}$ of this distance is $\frac{2}{3}$ of $\frac{1}{8}$ times the distance from Albany to Rome; what is the distance to Rome?

53. Fort-Plain is 56 miles from Albany, and $\frac{5}{7}$ of this distance is $1\frac{3}{5}$ times $\frac{1}{10}$ of the distance from Albany to Rochester; what is the distance to Rochester?

54. Waterloo is 192 miles from Albany, and $\frac{8}{9}$ of this distance is $1\frac{2}{3}$ times the distance from Albany

to Utica, and 3 miles more; what is the distance to Utica?

55. Buffalo is 325 miles from Albany, and $\frac{2}{5}$ of this distance is $7\frac{1}{2}$ times $\frac{1}{11}$ of the distance to Batavia, and 5 miles more; what is the distance from Albany to Batavia?

Distance on the Railroad between Albany and Boston.

56. Boston is 200 miles from Albany, and $\frac{2}{5}$ of this distance is $1\frac{3}{5}$ times $\frac{1}{4}$ of the distance to West Springfield; what is the distance to West Springfield?

57. From Albany to the State line is 38 miles, and $1\frac{1}{2}$ times this distance is $4\frac{3}{4}$ times $\frac{1}{9}$ the distance to Wilbraham; what is the distance to Wilbraham?

58. Kinderhook is 16 miles from Albany, and $\frac{3}{4}$ of this distance is $\frac{2}{3}$ times $\frac{1}{3}$ of the distance to Dalton; what is the distance to Dalton?

59. Brighton is 195 miles from Albany, and $\frac{2}{5}$ of this distance is $\frac{1}{4}$ of 2 times the distance to Worcester; what is the distance to Worcester?

60. Grafton is 162 miles from Albany, and $\frac{5}{9}$ of this distance is $\frac{1}{3}$ of 3 times the distance to Westfield, less 2 miles; how far is it to Westfield?

Lesson XIX.

1. $\frac{2}{3}$ of 9 is $\frac{3}{5}$ of how many times $\frac{1}{5}$ of 25?
2. $\frac{3}{4}$ of 16 is $\frac{1}{3}$ of how many times $\frac{1}{4}$ of 21?
3. $\frac{4}{5}$ of 40 is $\frac{2}{3}$ of how many times $\frac{1}{4}$ of 16?
4. $\frac{7}{8}$ of 80 is $\frac{2}{5}$ of how many times $\frac{1}{9}$ of 21?
5. $\frac{3}{4}$ of 36 is $\frac{1}{3}$ of how many times $\frac{3}{4}$ of 12?
6. $\frac{2}{9}$ of 45 is $\frac{2}{7}$ of how many times $\frac{5}{6}$ of 14?
7. $\frac{5}{6}$ of 30 is $\frac{5}{9}$ of how many times $\frac{1}{2}$ of 10?
8. $1\frac{1}{2}$ of 48 is $\frac{1}{5}$ of how many times $\frac{3}{4}$ of 7?
9. $\frac{4}{5}$ of 45 is $\frac{2}{3}$ of how many times $\frac{3}{4}$ of 8?

SOLUTION.—$\frac{4}{5}$ of 45 is 36. 36 is $\frac{2}{9}$ of 162. $\frac{3}{4}$ of 8 is 6. 162 is 27 times 6.

10. $\frac{5}{7}$ of 35 is $\frac{1}{7}$ of how many times $\frac{3}{7}$ of $11\frac{2}{3}$?
11. $\frac{7}{9}$ of 54 is $\frac{2}{3}$ of how many times $\frac{2}{3}$ of $10\frac{1}{2}$?
12. $\frac{3}{5}$ of 25 is $\frac{3}{4}$ of how many times $\frac{2}{5}$ of 10?
13. $\frac{4}{7}$ of 28 is $\frac{1}{5}$ of how many times $\frac{4}{5}$ of 25?
14. $\frac{4}{9}$ of 18 is $\frac{2}{9}$ of how many times $\frac{3}{4}$ of 12?
15. $\frac{5}{6}$ of 36 is $\frac{3}{11}$ of how many times $\frac{5}{6}$ of 12?
16. $\frac{4}{7}$ of 54 is $\frac{2}{4}$ of how many times $\frac{3}{4}$ of 16?
17. $\frac{7}{8}$ of 32 is $\frac{3}{4}$ of how many times $\frac{2}{3}$ of 9?
18. $\frac{8}{9}$ of 108 is $\frac{2}{3}$ of how many times $\frac{2}{3}$ of $\frac{2}{5}$ of 15?
19. $\frac{3}{4}$ of 40 is $\frac{5}{12}$ of how many times $\frac{1}{2}$ of $\frac{4}{5}$ of 20?
20. $\frac{4}{5}$ of 20 is $\frac{2}{5}$ of how many times $\frac{2}{3}$ of $\frac{3}{4}$ of 12?

Lesson XX.

1. If 1 horse eat $\frac{1}{4}$ of a bushel of oats in 1 day, now many horses will eat a bushel in the same time?

2. If the wages of 8 weeks amount to $48, what will the wages of $2\frac{3}{4}$ weeks amount to?

3. A ship's crew of 12 men have provision for 5 months; how many months will it last 5 men?

4. A man gained $14 by selling a watch for $1\frac{2}{5}$ times what it cost him; how much did it cost him?

5. There is a pole, $\frac{7}{9}$ of its length is under water, and 9 feet out; how long is the pole?

6. A pole is standing in the water, so that 15 feet is above the water, which is $\frac{3}{7}$ of the whole length of the pole; how long is the pole?

7. If $\frac{2}{3}$ be 2 what will 2 be?

8. If 8 horses can in 1 day eat 4 bushels of oats, in how many days can 1 horse eat 1 bushel?

9. If 3 horses can in 1 day eat $1\frac{1}{5}$ bushels of oats, how many bushels can 1 horse eat in 4 days?

10. If 1 horse in 2 days can eat 6 bushels of corn, how many bushels will 4 horses eat in 3 days?

11. If 4 horses eat 16 bushels of grain in 2 days, how many bushels will 3 horses eat in 12 days?

12. How many tons of hay will 3 horses consume in 4 days, if 4 horses in $\frac{1}{2}$ of a day consume $\frac{4}{5}$ of a ton?

13. How many hundred weight of hay can 3 horses consume in 25 days, if 2 horses in $\frac{1}{4}$ of a day consume $\frac{7}{400}$ of a hundred weight?

14. In how many days can 4 men cut 16 cords of wood, if 1 man in 1 day cut $\frac{1}{3}$ of a cord?

15. How many men will be required to earn 20 dimes in 4 days, if 4 men in $2\frac{3}{4}$ days earn 11 dimes?

16. If it require 6 days for 2 men to lay 36 rods of wall, how many men can in $\frac{1}{2}$ of the time build 72 rods of similar wall?

17. If in 4 days 3 men accomplish a certain piece of work, how many men will be required to perform a piece of work 4 times as large in 2 days?

18. If 4 men in 8 days perform a certain piece of work, how many men will be required to accomplish 3 times as much work in $\frac{3}{4}$ of a day?

19. If 1 horse eat 1 bushel of oats in 4 days, in how many days would 6 horses eat 48 bushels?

20. If $\frac{2}{3}$ of 6 be 3, what will $\frac{1}{5}$ of 40 be?

21. If 3 be $\frac{2}{3}$ of 6, what will $\frac{1}{5}$ of 40 be?

22. If 2 men in $\frac{1}{3}$ of a day earn $\frac{5}{12}$ of a dollar, in how many days can 3 men earn $\frac{3}{4}$ of a dollar?

23. If it require $\frac{1}{8}$ of a bushel of oats to feed 4 horses $\frac{1}{3}$ of a day, how many horses would it require to consume 9 bushels in $\frac{3}{5}$ of a day?

☞ SUGGESTION.—*Review unless the pupils thoroughly understand the preceding Chapters.*

The study of Chapter VII. may be omitted until the class has learned Chapter VIII., (excepting the miscellaneous questions.)

CHAPTER VII.

Lesson I.

1. $24 is $\frac{3}{5}$ of twice as much as a cask of wine cost; what did the wine cost?

2. Bought 30 barrels of flour, and $\frac{4}{5}$ of the number of barrels equalled $\frac{1}{5}$ as many dollars as they all cost; what did 1 barrel cost?

3. 35 is $\frac{5}{8}$ of how many times $\frac{2}{3}$ of 4?

4. A farmer being asked how many sheep he had, answered, that 160 was $\frac{2}{5}$ of 10 times his number; how how many sheep had he?

5. Mr. B, being asked the value of his horse, said, $54 is $\frac{6}{11}$ of 3 times its value; what is the value of his horse?

6. 72 is $\frac{8}{9}$ of how many times $\frac{3}{4}$ of 12?

7. 36 is $\frac{3}{4}$ of how many times $\frac{2}{3}$ of 12?

8. 48 is $\frac{2}{3}$ of how many times $\frac{1}{7}$ of 18?

9. 56 is $\frac{5}{9}$ of how many times $\frac{7}{8}$ of 8?

10. 60 is $\frac{3}{5}$ of how many times $\frac{5}{8}$ of 16?

11. 84 is $\frac{12}{5}$ of how many times $\frac{1}{5}$ of 25?

12. A spent $60, which was $\frac{5}{8}$ of 4 times as much as he was worth; how much was he worth?

13. B sold 9 sheep, which was $\frac{3}{10}$ times $\frac{1}{5}$ of his whole flock; how many sheep had he remaining?

14. D, at a game of cards, lost $20, which was $\frac{4}{7}$ times $\frac{5}{8}$ of all the money he had; how much had he?

15. C found $45, which was $\frac{5}{9}$ of 3 times as much as he already had; how much more did he find than he had at first?

16. A boy lost 9 marbles, which was $\frac{3}{8}$ of twice as many as he had at first; how many had he left?

17. A boy gave away 8 apples, which was $\frac{4}{7}$ of

twice as many as he had left; how many had he at first?

18. 12 is $\frac{3}{5}$ times $\frac{3}{7}$ of what number?

19. 36 is $\frac{6}{11}$ times $\frac{2}{5}$ of how many times $\frac{3}{4}$ of $13\frac{1}{3}$?

20. Jeremiah is 18 years old, and his age is $\frac{3}{4}$ times $\frac{2}{3}$ of his father's age; how old is his father?

21. Mary gave 6 cents for a comb, which was $\frac{2}{5}$ times $\frac{1}{2}$ of all her money; how many cents had she?

22. Martha gave 8 cents for a pine-apple, which was $\frac{2}{7}$ times $\frac{2}{3}$ of all her money; how many apples could she have bought with the money she had remaining, at 2 cents apiece?

23. Henry had 20 marbles, which was $\frac{2}{3}$ of twice as many as Harry had; how many had Harry?

24. Margaret is 16 years old, and her age is $\frac{2}{9}$ of 3 times Martha's age; how old is Martha?

25. $\frac{3}{4}$ is $\frac{2}{3}$ of twice as much as what number?

26. A man bought a horse for $60, which was $\frac{3}{7}$ of twice as much as he sold him for; how much did he gain by the bargain?

27. A horse was sold for $40, which was $\frac{4}{6}$ times $\frac{5}{6}$ of what he was worth; what was the value of the horse?

28. A man when he was married was 20 years of age, which was $\frac{5}{6}$ times $\frac{9}{7}$ of the age of his wife; how old was she?

29. Shepherd was worth $160, which was $\frac{4}{7}$ times $\frac{1}{16}$ of his father's fortune; what was his father's fortune?

30. A and B were playing cards; B lost $14, which was $\frac{7}{10}$ times $\frac{2}{3}$ as much as A then had; and when they commenced $\frac{5}{8}$ of A's money equalled $\frac{2}{7}$ of B's. How much had each when they began to play?

31. A and B were playing cards, A lost $20, which was $\frac{5}{14}$ of the number of dollars B then had more than A; provided this sum was $1\frac{1}{6}$ times as much as A had at first, how much had each when they began to play?

Lesson II.

1. A boy, after spending $\frac{3}{5}$ of all his money, found that 16 cents was all he had remaining; how much had he at first?

SOLUTION.—Let $\frac{5}{5}$ equal the money he had at first. Then after spending $\frac{3}{5}$ of it, he had remaining $\frac{5}{5}-\frac{3}{5}$, which is $\frac{2}{5}$. This by the condition of the question is 16 cents. If $\frac{2}{5}$ of the money he had at first is 16 cents, $\frac{1}{5}$ of it is $\frac{1}{2}$ of 16 cents, which is 8 cents; and $\frac{5}{5}$, or what he had at first, are five times 8, or 40 cents.

SOLUTION 2nd.—He spent $\frac{3}{5}$ of his money; therefore, he had remaining $\frac{2}{5}$ of it, which equals 16 cents. If $\frac{2}{5}$ of his money is 16 cents, he must have had 40 cents.

2. Ruth, after losing $\frac{2}{3}$ of all her roses, had only 3 remaining; how many had she at first?

3. Jane gave $\frac{3}{5}$ of all her flowers to Ann, and had 4 remaining; how many did she give to Ann?

4. George, after eating $\frac{9}{13}$ of all his oranges, had only 8 oranges remaining; how many had he at first?

5. A boy expended $\frac{1}{9}$ of his money for a pie, $\frac{2}{9}$ for a ball, $\frac{3}{9}$ for a top, and had 6 cents remaining; how many cents had he at first?

6. In a certain school $\frac{1}{2}$ of the scholars study grammar, $\frac{1}{3}$ study arithmetic, and the remainder, which is 10, study geography; how many scholars in all, and how many attending to each study?

7. A third part of an army was killed, $\frac{1}{4}$ part taken prisoners, and 300 escaped; how many were there in the army?

8. If from my age you subtract $\frac{1}{2}$ and $\frac{2}{5}$ of my age the remainder is 2 years; how old am I?

9. B, being asked how many pigeons he caught, said, that if to $\frac{5}{9}$ of the number 36 were added, the sum would equal twice the number. How many did he catch?

10. If to $\frac{3}{4}$ of the cost of B's horse you add $100, the sum will be twice the cost of the horse ; what was the cost of the horse?

11. A gentleman, after spending $\frac{3}{7}$ of his fortune, and $\frac{1}{2}$ of the remainder, had $2400 remaining; what was his fortune?

12. A gambler lost $\frac{3}{4}$ of all his money, and the next night he won $\frac{2}{3}$ as much as he lost the night before; he then had $90; how much had he at first?

13. John had stolen from him $\frac{5}{7}$ of his money, and the thief was not caught until he had spent $\frac{5}{7}$ of it; the remainder, which was $40 less than John had remaining, was given back; how much money had John at first?

14. A traveller had stolen from him $\frac{5}{7}$ of all his money, and the thief was not caught until he had spent $\frac{1}{3}$ of it, the remainder ($100) was given back; how much had he at first?

15. If to $\frac{1}{2}$ of the cost of A's watch you add $10, the sum will be $21 ; what was the cost of his watch?

16. If to $\frac{2}{5}$ of B's age you add 15 years, the sum would be 39 years ; how old is B?

17. A drover being asked how many sheep he had, said, if to $\frac{1}{3}$ of my flock you add the number $9\frac{1}{2}$, the sum will be $99\frac{1}{2}$; how many sheep had he ?

18. $\frac{5}{7}$ of the length of a pole is in the water, and 12 feet in the air; how long is the pole?

19. If to $\frac{7}{8}$ of A's age you add 16 years, the sum will be $1\frac{1}{8}$ times his age; how old is he?

20. A man, being asked how many pigeons he caught, replied, if to $\frac{3}{4}$ of the number I caught you add 20, the sum would lack 4 of being equal to $1\frac{1}{2}$ times the number ; how many did he catch?

8

Lesson III.

1. Divide the number 36 into two parts, which shall be to each other as 7 to 2.

SOLUTION.—Since the two parts are to be to each other as 7 to 2, we must divide 36 into 7 + 2, which are 9 equal parts; and 7 of the parts will be one of the numbers, and 2 of them the other. ⅑ of 36 is 4, and ⁷/₉ are 7 times 4, which are 28 (the first number,) and ²/₉ are 2 times 4, which are 8 (the other number). Or, in the latter part of the solution, say: ⁷/₉ of 36 is 28, the first number; and ²/₉ of 36 is 8, the other number.

2. Two men hired a pasture for $72; one put in 7 horses, and the other 2 horses; what ought each to pay?

3. A and B hired a pasture for $14; A put in 4 cows, and B put in 3 cows; what ought each to pay?

4. A and B bought a lottery ticket for $5; A paid $3, and B paid $2. They drew a prize of $60; what was each one's share?

5. Two men bought 40 mules; the first paid $5 as often as the other $3. How many mules ought each to receive?

6. Mary and Elizabeth went to school 80 days, and as often as Mary went 3 days, Elizabeth went 5 days; how many days did each go?

7. Reuben had 7 cents, and Blake 4 cents; they paid all their money for 22 apples; how many ought each to receive?

8. Three men bought a lottery ticket for $12; the first paid $2, the second $7, and the third $3. They drew a prize of $240; what was each man's share?

9. Three men hired a pasture for $24; the first put in 2 horses, the second put in 3 horses, and the third put in 4 horses; how much ought each to pay?

10. A man, failing in business, was able to pay only ⅘ of his debts; how much will that man receive to whom he owes $90?

11. A man, meeting an equal number of poor women

and boys, gave to each woman 7 dimes, and to each boy 2 dimes; and to them all he gave $9; how many women and boys were there respectively?

12. Two men bought a barrel of fish for $9; the first paid $4, the second $5; what part of the barrel belongs to each?

13. A farmer gave 35 bushels of rye to two of his poor neighbors; to the first he gave 1 bushel as often as to the other ¾ of a bushel; how many bushels did each receive?

14. Three men hired a pasture for $36; the first put in 3 horses, the second 2 horses, and the third 4 horses; how much ought each to pay?

15. Two men hired a pasture for $60; the first put in 4 horses for two weeks, and the second put in 3 horses for 4 weeks; how much ought each to pay?

16. Three men hired a pasture for $15; the first put in 4 sheep for 5 weeks, the second put in 8 sheep for 5 weeks, and the third put in 10 sheep for 9 weeks; how much ought each to pay?

17. Two men entered into partnership; the first put in $40 for 10 months, and the second put in $80 for 5 months; they gained $95; what was each man's share of the gain?

18. A and B agreed to cut a field of wheat for $20; A sent 5 men for 4 days, and B sent 3 men for 10 days; how much ought each to receive?

19. Divide $56 between A and B, giving to A $1 as often as to B ⅖ of a dollar.

20. A and B hired a pasture for $24; a put in 4 sheep for 10 weeks, and B put in 2 horses for 10 weeks; what ought each to pay provided 2 sheep in 1 week eat as much as a horse in the same time?

21. Simpson, Domer, and Eyer, enter into a joint speculation by which they clear $460. Simpson claims to have furnished ¾, Domer ⅔, and Eyer ½ of the entire capital. How much according to these calculations ought each to receive?

Lesson IV.

1. B had 4 apples more than A, and tney together had 14 ; how many had each ?

SOLUTION.—By a condition of the question B's number is equal to A's + 4 apples; to which add A's number, and we have 2 times A's number + 4=14. Therefore, 2 times A's number equals 14—4, or 10 ; and once his number equals ½ of 10, or 5 apples. And B's number is 5 + 4 = 9 apples.

2. Heman has 6 books more than Handford, and both have 26; how many has each?

3. Robert has 7 marbles more than Richard, and both have 35; how many has each?

4. Mary has 4 roses more than Martha, and both have 24; how many has each?

5. Alice has 7 pins more than Abner, and both have 29 ; how many has each ?

6. $\frac{2}{5}$ of $\frac{2}{3}$ is $\frac{4}{5}$ of what number?

7. The sum of two numbers is 36, and their difference is 16 ; what are the two numbers?

8. A boy bought $\frac{5}{7}$ of a melon for $8\frac{1}{3}$ cents ; how much is that apiece ?

9 Homer and Hannah each bought an equal number of peaches ; on their way home Hannah had 4 more given to her, then they together had 24; how many did each buy?

10. Two boys had each an equal number of blocks; one lost 4 of his; and together they then had only 12 remaining ; how many had each at first?

11. A wagon was sold for $17\frac{2}{3}$, which was $\frac{2}{3}$ as much as it cost; what did it cost ?

12. Hiram had twice as many strawberries as Eugene, and both had 18 pints ; how many had each?

13. Ida had 6 cents more than twice as many as Ira, and both had 36 ; how many had each?

14. Susan had $\frac{1}{5}$ as many cents as Sarah ; Sarah

lost 10 of hers; then together they had 50; how many had each at first?

15. Thomas was returning from market with twice as many eggs as Timothy; Thomas broke 4 of his, and Timothy 6 of his; they then had 40 eggs remaining; how many had each at first?

16. $\frac{3}{5}$ of a number $+$ 14 $=$ 44; what is that number?

17. A boy being asked his age, replied, 3 times my age—7 years are 23 years. How old was he?

18. A, being asked how much money he had, replied, twice what I have $+$ $60, is four times $400; how much money had A?

19. Two boys had 49 marbles, but the first has 7 the most; how many has each?

20. A man bought a sheep, a cow, and a horse for $70; the cow cost $10 more than the sheep, and the horse cost $20 more than the cow. What was the cost of each?

21. A man bought a melon for $18\frac{3}{4}$ cents, which was only $\frac{3}{5}$ as much as his dinner cost; what was the cost of his dinner?

22. A gentleman bought a watch and chain for $80; the chain cost $\frac{1}{3}$ as much as the watch; what was the cost of each?

23. A farmer bought a plough, a harness, and a horse for $58 ; for the harness he gave $6 more than for the plough, and for the horse $34 more than for the harness. How much did he give for each?

24. A boy bought twice as many oranges as lemons, and on his way home ate 4 oranges and gave 6 away, and was surprised to find he had only 14 oranges remaining. How many of each kind did he buy?

25. 5 times a certain number—12 is 48; what is that number?

26. $\frac{3}{4}$ of a certain number—5 is 40; what is that number?

27. A boy, being asked his age, replied, 11 years are 7 years more than $\frac{2}{5}$ of my age; how old was he?

28. A boy, being asked how many sheep his father had, replied, 40 are 5 less than $\frac{3}{4}$ of his number. How many had he?

29. A boy bought 18 lemons;—for $\frac{2}{3}$ of them he paid 3 cents for 2, and for the remainder he paid 3 cents apiece; for what must he sell them apiece to gain 10 cents on the whole?

30. James, John and Joseph, together have 96 peaches; James has 2 more than John, and Joseph has as many as both James and John ; how many has each ?

31. Henry bought 54 oranges; for $\frac{2}{3}$ of them he paid 2 cents for 3, and for the remainder, 3 cents for 2; and sold $\frac{1}{3}$ of them, at the rate of 2 cents for 3, and the remainder at 3 cents for 2.   How much did he gain by so doing?

Lesson V.

1. If a man can do a certain piece of work in 12 days, what part of it can he do in 1 day?

2. If a man can drink a barrel of beer in 20 weeks, what part of it can he drink in 1 week?

3. If it require 9 hours to empty a vessel, what part of it can be emptied in 1 hour ?

4. If a family consume a barrel of pork in 30 days, whar part of a barrel do they daily consume?

5. If it require 19 days to perform a certain journey, what part of it can be performed in 1 day ?

6. If A can do a certain piece of work in 8 days, and B could do the same in 12 days, what part of it can each do in a day ?

7. If C could mow a certain field in 4 days, and D could do the same in 6 days, what part of it could

each do in a day, and how much could they together do in a day?

8. If C and D can, in 1 day, mow $\frac{5}{12}$ of a field, how long would it take them to mow the whole field?

9. How many days would it take to perform a certain piece of work, if $\frac{3}{15}$ of it can be performed in 1 day?

10. If George can do a certain piece of work in 3 days, and Granvil in 6 days; how long will it take them together to do the work?

11. If James can eat a bushel of apples in 10 days, and Rud in 12 days, how long would 1 bushel last both?

12. A can cut a field of wheat in 12 days, and B can do the same in 20 days; how long would it take them to cut the field when they work together?

13. A merchant bought a hogshead of molasses for $20, 10 gallons of which leaked out; how must he sell the remainder a gallon to gain $6.50.

14. If $\frac{2}{3}$ of a barrel of flour cost 4\frac{2}{3}$, what will $\frac{4}{5}$ of a barrel cost?

15. A and B can build a boat in 20 days, and with the assistance of C, they can build it in 8 days. How long would it take C to do it alone?

16. A farmer and his son can do a piece of work in 6 days; the son can do the same in 27 days. How long would it take the father to do the work?

17. Three pipes, A, B, and C, can fill a cistern in 2 hours, A and B can fill it in 4 hours, and A and C can fill it in 3 hours. How long would it take each to fill it?

18. If a barrel of beer would last a man 35 days, and the man and his son 20 days, how long would it last the son alone?

19. A box of tea, usually, lasted a man and his wife 9 months; when the man was absent it would last the wife 12 months. How long would it have lasted the man alone?

20. A, B, and C can build a boat in 20 days, A and B, in 40 days, and A and C, in 30 days. How long would it take each separately to build it?

21. Provided A could drink a barrel of beer in 24 days, and B in 36 days, how long would it take them together to drink a barrel, after $\frac{3}{8}$ of it had leaked out?

22. A market-woman bought 30 oranges, and had $\frac{1}{3}$ of them stolen; the remainder she sold at 3 cents each, and thereby gained $\frac{2}{3}$ of a cent on each orange bought. How much did they cost apiece?

23. A can do a certain piece of work in $4\frac{1}{2}$ days, and A and B together, in 3 days. After A did $\frac{1}{2}$ of the work, B did the remainder; how long did it take him?

24. If a man can do a certain piece of work in $\frac{2}{3}$ of a day, how much can he do in 1 day?

25. If a man can chop a cord of wood in $\frac{3}{7}$ of a day, how much can he chop in 1 day?

26. Isaac can make a pair of boots in $\frac{2}{3}$ of a day, and Ira in $\frac{2}{5}$ of a day; how many pair can both make in 1 day?

27. Samuel can cut a cord of wood in $\frac{3}{4}$ of a day, and Theodore in $\frac{2}{5}$ of a day; how long would it take them to cut a cord, when they worked together?

28. If $\frac{2}{5}$ of an apple cost $\frac{6}{7}$ of a cent, what will $\frac{5}{6}$ of an apple cost?

29. A can mow 1 acre of grass in $\frac{2}{3}$ of a day, B, in $\frac{3}{4}$ of a day, and C, in $\frac{4}{5}$ of a day. How much more can A and B mow in a day than C?

30. If a wolf can eat a sheep in $\frac{7}{8}$ of an hour, and a bear can eat it in $\frac{3}{4}$ of an hour, how long would it take them together to eat what remained of a sheep after the wolf had been eating $\frac{1}{2}$ of an hour?

Lesson VI.

1. Lewis, meeting some beggars, gave each of them 2 cents, and had 12 cents remaining; if he had given them 4 cents each, it would have taken all the money he had. How many beggars were there?

SOLUTION.— By the last condition of the question, he gave each beggar 2 cents more than by the first, and to them all 12 cents *more* than by the first condition. Therefore there must have been as many beggars as 2 is contained times in 12, which are 6 beggars.

2. A boy gave to each of his playmates 3 cents, and had 24 cents remaining; if he had given them each 7 cents, it would have taken all the money he had. How many playmates had he?

3. Mary gave each of her playmates 5 apples; if she had given them each 7 apples it would have taken 12 apples more; how many playmates had she?

4. A certain number of persons gave me 10 cents each; had they given me 12 cents each it would have amounted to 20 cents more; how many persons were there?

5. $\frac{3}{5}$ of $100 is $\frac{3}{250}$ of $\frac{1}{5}$ times the salary of the President of the United States. What is his salary?

6. $40 is $\frac{2}{7}$ of $\frac{1}{80}$ of the salary of the Vice-President of the United States. What is his salary?

7. Divide 35 oranges between James and Joseph, so that James may have 15 more than Joseph.

8. A cask of wine was sold for $96, which was $\frac{3}{4}$ of twice as much as it cost; how much did it cost?

9. By selling a quantity of cotton for $560, I gained $\frac{3}{4}$ of what it cost; how much did it cost?

10. A and B are 187 miles apart, and are travelling towards each other; one at the rate of 8 miles an hour, and the other 9 miles an hour; how many hours before they will meet?

11. Agnes gave 2 dimes a yard for a piece of calico; had she given 3 dimes a yard it would have cost her 20 dimes more; how many yards did the piece contain?

12. A was ordered to buy a certain number of oranges; if he bought those at 2 cents each, he would have had no money left,—had he bought those at 3 cents each, he would have wanted 10 cents more to have paid for them. How many oranges was he required to buy?

13. A lady wished to buy a certain number of yards of muslin; there were two kinds, some at 9 cents a yard, and some at 12 cents a yard. Had she taken that at 12 cents a yard it would have cost 36 cents more than the other kind. How many yards did she wish to buy?

14. A boy being sent to market to buy a certain number of pounds of meat, found, if he bought beef, at 5 cents a pound, he would have 39 cents remaining, but if he bought pork, at 8 cents a pound, he would have only 6 cents remaining. For how much meat was he sent?

15. If 8 times a certain number is 36 more than 5 times the same number, what is that number?

16. A boy being asked his age, said, 4 times my age is 24 years more than 2 times my age; how old was he?

17. A boy, being asked how many sheets of paper he had, said, 4 times the number is 18 less than 7 times the number; how many sheets of paper had he?

18. A person wishing to buy some butter, found, if he bought that which was 10 cents a pound, he would have 20 cents remaining; but if he bought that which was 12 cents a pound, he would lack 14 cents of having money enough to pay for it. How many pounds did he wish to buy?

19. A farmer, wishing to buy a certain number of sheep, found, if he gave $2 a head, he would have $20

remaining; but if he gave $5 a head he would lack $40 of having money enough to pay for them. How many sheep did he wish to buy?

20. A, B, and C, talking of their ages; says A to B, I am 4 times as old as you; says B to C I am $\frac{1}{2}$ as old as you, but says A to C, I am 40 years older than you. Required the ages of each?

Lesson VII.

1. A laborer agreed to work 40 days upon this condition; that for every day he worked he should receive $2, and for every day he was idle he should pay $1 for his board. At the expiration of the time, he received $50. How many days did he work?

SOLUTION.—If he had labored the whole time, he would have received 40 times $2, or $80. But he received only $50: he, therefore, lost by his idleness $80—$50, or $30. For every day he was idle he lost $2 (his daily wages) + $1 (the cost of his board) which are $3. If in 1 day he lose $3, he will lose $1 in $\frac{1}{3}$ of a day, and $30 in 30 times $\frac{1}{3}$ of a day, or 10 days. Therefore he was idle 10 days, and worked 40—10 days, or 30 days.

2. A man agreed to work 60 days on this condition; that for every day he worked he should receive $1\frac{1}{2}$, and for every day he was idle he should pay $\frac{1}{2}$ for his board. At the expiration of the time he received $68. How many days did he work?

3. A man was hired for 80 days on this condition; that for every day he worked he should receive 6 dimes, and for every day he was idle, he should forfeit 4 dimes. At the expiration of the time he received $40. How many days did he work?

4. How many times $\frac{2}{3}$ of 12 is $\frac{7}{8}$ of 40?

5. A and B bought a quantity of flour for $50; A paid $1 as often as B $\frac{2}{3}$ of a dollar; what part of the flour belongs to each?

6. A, B, and C built a house, which cost $500, of which B paid $100 more than A, and C paid as much as A and B both; how much did each pay?

7. A merchant sold a quantity of cloth for $84, and thereby lost $\frac{2}{5}$ of what it cost; what did it cost?

8. $7\frac{1}{2}$ is $2\frac{1}{2}$ times $\frac{2}{3}$ of how many times $1\frac{1}{4}$?

9. A farmer having in his employ an equal number of men and boys, to each boy he gave $4, to each man $8; and to them all he gave $84; how many men were there?

10. Two men hired a pasture for $35; one put in 3 cows, and the other put in 4; how much ought each to pay?

11. A man sold an equal number of ducks and turkeys for 20 dimes; the ducks, at 2 dimes each, and the turkeys at 3 dimes each; how many did he sell in all?

12. A farmer sold an equal number of ducks and turkeys; the ducks at 4 dimes each, the turkeys at 7 dimes each; and for the turkeys he received $3 more than for the ducks; how many of each kind did he sell?

13. There are two baskets, containing 37 apples; in one of which there are 17 more than in the other; how many apples are there in each?

14. Charles and Henry together have 49 marbles, and Charles has 7 more than twice as many as Henry; how many has each?

15. Philip has 20 apples more than Philo; and together they have 92; how many has each?

16. Three boys have 47 lemons; the first has 3 more than the second, and the second has 7 more than the third; how many has each?

17. A boy was hired for 20 days, on this condition, that for every day he labored, he should receive 3 dimes, and for every day he was idle, should pay 2 dimes for his board. At the expiration

of the time he received only $1. How many days was he idle?

18. A boy bought a whistle, a whip, and a drum for 70 cents. For the whip he gave twice as much as for the drum, and for the drum, twice as much as for the whistle; how much did he give for each?

19. The sum of 3 numbers is 54. The first is twice, and the third 3 times the second; what are those numbers?

20. Sarah's age is $\frac{2}{3}$ of Susan's, and the sum of their ages is 25; what is the age of each?

21. $\frac{5}{9}$ of an army were killed, $\frac{2}{3}$ of the remainder taken prisoners, and 400 escaped. How many were there in the army?

Lesson VIII.

1. A fishing rod, the length of which was 14 feet, was broken into two pieces. The shorter piece was $\frac{3}{4}$ of the length of the longer. What was the length of each piece?

SOLUTION.—$\frac{3}{4}$ of the length of the longer piece, which is the length of the shorter, $+ \frac{4}{4}$ (the length of the longer) $= \frac{7}{4}$ of the length of the longer, which is the length of both, or 14 feet. If $\frac{7}{4}$ of the longer is 14 feet, $\frac{1}{4}$ is $\frac{1}{7}$ of 14 feet, which is 2 feet, and $\frac{4}{4}$ (which is the length of the longer) are 4 times 2 feet, or 8 feet. 14—8 = 6 feet, the length of the shorter piece.

2. A pole, the length of which is 20 feet, is in the air and water, $\frac{2}{3}$ of the length in the air equals the length in the water; what is the length in the air and water respectively?

3. If in 2 days a man travelled 160 miles, and $\frac{3}{5}$ of the distance he travelled the first day equals the distance he travelled the second day, how far did he travel each day?

4. B and C together have 40 marbles; how many has each, provided $\frac{2}{3}$ of B's number is equal to C's?

5. From New York City to Redhook is 100 miles, and $\frac{1}{3}$ of the distance from New York to Rhinebeck, equals the distance from Rhinebeck to Redhook. How far from Rhinebeck to New York, and how far from Rhinebeck to Redhook?

6. If a horse and a colt were worth $90, and the horse was worth $1\frac{1}{2}$ times as much as the colt; what was the value of each?

7. A boy paid 70 cents for a slate and a book; how much did he pay for each, provided the book cost $1\frac{1}{3}$ times as much as the slate?

8. If a traveller pay $1.20 for his breakfast and dinner, how much did he pay for each, provided his dinner cost $\frac{5}{7}$ as much as his breakfast?

9. A pole, the length of which is 67 feet, is in the air and water; $\frac{2}{3}$ of the length in the air + 7 feet equals the length in the water. Required the length in the air, and in the water?

10. Divide the number 108 into two such parts, that $\frac{3}{7}$ of the first + 8 shall equal the second.

11. Divide the number 97 into two such parts, that $\frac{3}{7}$ of the first + 7 shall equal the second.

12. There is a fish the length of which is 18 feet; its tail is 4 feet, and $\frac{2}{3}$ the length of the body equals the length of the head. What is the length of the head and body respectively?

13. There is a fish the weight of which is 11 pounds, and $\frac{1}{2}$ of the weight of the head + 8 pounds equals the weight of the body; what is the weight of each?

14. A ship-mast, 51 feet in length, was broken off in a storm, and $\frac{2}{3}$ of the length broken off equalled $\frac{3}{4}$ of the length remaining; how much was broken off, and how much remained?

15. A boy being asked how many apples and

oranges he had, answered, in all I have 36, and $\frac{2}{5}$ of the number of apples, equals $\frac{1}{2}$ of the number of oranges; how many of each kind had he?

16. $\frac{2}{3}$ of one number equals $\frac{3}{5}$ of another, and their sum is 57; what are the two numbers?

17. A farmer has 290 sheep in two different fields; and $\frac{3}{4}$ of the number in the first field equals $\frac{3}{7}$ of the number in the second; how many are there in each field?

18. A market woman was requested to buy 33 fowls, consisting of two kinds; $\frac{1}{4}$ of the number of the first kind was to equal $\frac{2}{3}$ of the number of the second; how many of each kind must she buy?

19. A person, being asked the time of day, said, the time past noon is $\frac{1}{7}$ of the time past midnight; what was the hour?

Remark.—Since the time past noon is $\frac{1}{7}$ of the time past midnight, the time from midnight to noon, which is 12 hours, must be $\frac{6}{7}$ of the time past midnight.

20. A person, being asked the hour of the day, said, the time past noon is $\frac{1}{3}$ of the time past midnight; what was the hour?

21. A person, being asked the hour of the day, said, the time past noon is $\frac{1}{3}$ of the time from now to midnight; what was the hour?

Solution.—From now to midnight is $\frac{3}{3}$, and $\frac{1}{3}$ added (the time past noon) is $\frac{4}{3}$. Consequently from noon to midnight (which is 12 hours) is $\frac{4}{3}$ of the time it lacked of being midnight; and $\frac{1}{4}$ of the time is $\frac{1}{4}$ of 12, which is 3 hours, the time past noon.

22. What is the time of day, provided $\frac{3}{4}$ of the time from now to midnight equals the time past noon?

23. A man, being asked the hour of the day, said, $\frac{2}{3}$ of the time past noon equals $\frac{2}{9}$ of the time from now to midnight; what was the time?

24. A pole, the length of which was 68 feet, was in the air and water; $\frac{3}{4}$ of the length in the air equalled

$\frac{2}{3}$ of the length in the water. What was the length in the air and in the water respectively?

25. The sum of two numbers is 176, and $\frac{3}{4}$ of the first $+$ 4 equals $\frac{2}{3}$ of the second; required the numbers.

26. A person, being asked the time of day, said $\frac{3}{5}$ of the time past midnight equals $\frac{3}{10}$ of the time from now to midnight again; what o'clock is it?

27. Provided the time past 10 o'clock, A. M., equals $\frac{3}{4}$ of the time to midnight, what o'clock is it?

28. Says A to B, $\frac{3}{4}$ of my age $+$ 4 years equals $\frac{2}{3}$ of yours, and the sum of our ages is 74 years. What is each of their ages?

29. A person, being asked the hour of the day, replied, $\frac{2}{3}$ of the time past noon equals $\frac{2}{9}$ of the time from now to midnight $+\frac{2}{3}$ hours; what was the time?

30. A pole, the length of which is 78 feet, is in the air and water; $\frac{9}{8}$ of the length in the air $+$ 12 feet, equals $1\frac{1}{4}$ times the length in the water. What is the length in the air and water respectively?

Lesson IX.

1. There is a fish the head of which is 4 inches long, and whose tail is as long as its head $+\frac{1}{2}$ of its body, and whose body is as long as its head and tail; what is the length of the fish?

SOLUTION.—By a condition of the question, $\frac{1}{2}$ of the length of body $+$ 4 inches, is the length of tail; to which add 4 inches, (the length of the head), and we have $\frac{1}{2}$ of the length of the body $+$ 8 inches $=\frac{2}{2}$, or the length of the body. Therefore, $\frac{2}{2}-\frac{1}{2}$ or $\frac{1}{2}$ of the length of the body, equals 8 inches; and $\frac{4}{2}$, or twice the length of the body, which is the length of the fish, equals 4 times 8 inches, or 32 inches.

2. The head of a fish is 6 inches long, its tail is as long as its head $+\frac{1}{2}$ of its body, and the body is as

long as the head and tail together; what is the length of the fish?

3. The head of a fish is 12 inches long, the tail is as long as the head + $\frac{1}{2}$ of the body, and the body is as long as the head and tail; what is the length of the fish?

4. The head of a fish weighs 10 pounds, the tail weighs as much as the head + $\frac{2}{3}$ as much as the body ; and the body weighs as much as the head and tail; what is the weight of the tail?

5. $\frac{5}{7}$ of a certain number equals $\frac{2}{7}$ of the same number + 10; what is that number?

6. A boy, being asked his age, replied, $\frac{2}{3}$ of my age exceeded $\frac{2}{5}$ of my age by 4 years; how old was he?

7. James, being asked how many arithmetical questions he had answered correctly during the week, replied, $\frac{3}{4}$ of the number is 3 more than $\frac{3}{8}$ of the number ; how many questions had he answered?

8. A farmer, after selling $\frac{2}{3}$ of $1\frac{1}{5}$ times as much grain as he had, had 80 bushels remaining; how much had he at first?

9. An individual, after spending $\frac{2}{3}$ of all his money, and $\frac{2}{3}$ of what then remained, had only $12\frac{2}{3}$ remaining; how much had he at first?

10. If $\frac{6}{7}$ of a ship be worth $\frac{4}{5}$ of her cargo, which is valued at 300 eagles, what is the value of the ship?

11. Dick being asked how much money he had, said, its $\frac{1}{2}$ exceeded its $\frac{3}{8}$ by $2; how much had he?

12. A tree, by falling, was broken into three pieces; the top part was 10 feet long, the bottom part was as long as the top + $\frac{3}{5}$ of the middle, and the middle part was as long as the other two ; what was the length of the tree, and of each piece?

13. A man bought a hat, a coat, and a watch; the hat cost $6, the watch cost as much as the hat + $\frac{2}{5}$ of

9

the cost of the coat, and the coat cost as much as the hat and watch; what was the cost of each, and of all?

14. $\frac{2}{3}$ of $\frac{3}{4}$ is how many times $\frac{2}{5}$ of $\frac{5}{16}$?

15. If $\frac{3}{4}$ of a ton of hay cost $\frac{3}{5}$ of an eagle, how many dollars will $\frac{1}{2}$ of a ton cost?

16. A third and $\frac{1}{2}$ of a third of 10 is $\frac{5}{8}$ of what number?

17. If from a certain number you take its $\frac{1}{2}$ and its $\frac{1}{3}$, the remainder will be $13\frac{2}{3}$; what is that number?

18. After spending $\frac{2}{3}$ of my money, I earned $\frac{2}{3}$ as much as I spent, and then had only $20 less than what I had at first; how much had I at first?

19. The head of a fish is 8 inches long, the tail is as long as the head and $\frac{1}{2}$ of the body + 10 inches, and the body is as long as the head and tail; what is the length of the fish?

20. The head of a fish is 12 inches long; its tail is 10 inches longer than its head increased by $\frac{1}{2}$ the length of the body; and its body is 20 inches longer than its head and tail together. What is the length of the fish?

Lesson X.

1. James is 20 years old, and John is 4 years old; in how many years will James, who is now 5 times as old as John, be only twice as old?

REMARK.—Four years ago James was 16, and in 16 years more he will be twice as old as John.

2. Sarah is 10 years old, and Sally is 4; in how many years will Sally be $\frac{1}{2}$ as old as Sarah?

3. Jacob is 40 years old, and Alfred is 2; in how many years will Alfred be $\frac{1}{4}$ as old as Jacob?

4. If the third of 6 be 3, what will $\frac{1}{4}$ of 20 be?

5. If 3 be the third of 6, what will the $\frac{1}{4}$ of 20 be?

6. If $\frac{2}{3}$ of 12 be 10, what will $\frac{2}{3}$ of 10 be?

7. Divide the number 85 into two parts, that shall be to each other as $\frac{2}{3}$ to $\frac{3}{4}$.

8. When A was married, he was 3 times as old as his wife, but when they had been married 15 years, he was only twice as old as she; how old was each when they were married?

REMARK.—The conditions of the above question give the following:

9. Three times a certain number + 15 equals twice the same number + 30; what is that number, and what is 3 times the same number?

10. Once a certain number + 15 equals $\frac{2}{3}$ of the same number + 30; what is that number, and what is $\frac{1}{3}$ of the same number?

11. When I first met Mr. A, I was $\frac{1}{3}$ as old as he was, and in 12 years after that, I was $\frac{3}{4}$ as old as he was; what was each of our ages when we first met?

12. There are two numbers, one of which is 4 times the other; but if to each 20 were added, one will be double the other; what are these numbers?

13. When B was married he was 3 times as old as his wife; but after they had been married 60 years, $\frac{2}{3}$ of his age equalled hers; what was the age of each when they were married?

14. A hound takes 3 leaps to a fox's 4, and 3 of the hound's leaps are equal to 6 of the fox's; how many leaps must the hound take to gain 1 on the fox?

15. If the hound takes $1\frac{1}{2}$ leaps to gain 1 on the fox, how many must he take to gain 20 on the fox?

16. A hare is 20 leaps before a hound, and takes 4 leaps to the hound's 3; and 3 of the hound's leaps are equal to 6 of the hare's. How many leaps must the hound take to catch the hare?

17. A fox is 60 leaps before a hound, and takes 5 leaps to the hound's 2; and 4 of the hound's leaps equal 12 of the fox's. How many leaps must the hound take to catch the fox?

18. Alfred is 60 steps before Silas, and takes 9 steps to Silas's 6; and 3 of Silas's steps equal 7 of Alfred's. How many steps, at this rate, will each take before they will be together?

REMARK.—*A box of glass contains* 50 *square feet, or as nearly as may be.*

19. How many panes of glass in a box, provided they are 6 by 8 inches?

REMARK.—Find the area of a pane of glass by reducing the inches to parts of a foot, and then multiply these parts together. The area of a pane 6 by 8 inches is $\frac{1}{3}$ of a square foot. The remainder may be solved as follows:

SOLUTION.—If to make $\frac{1}{3}$ of a square foot it require 1 pane, to make $\frac{3}{3}$, or 1 square foot, it will require 3 times 1, or 3 panes; and to make 50 square feet, (1 box,) it will require 50 times 3 panes, which are 150 panes.

20. How many panes of glass in a box, provided they are 8 by 10 inches?

21. How many panes of glass in a box, provided they are 10 by 12 inches?

22. How many panes of glass in a box, provided they are 8 by 12 inches?

23. How many panes of glass in a box, provided they are 12 by 15 inches?

Lesson XI.

1. What number is that, to which if its $\frac{1}{2}$ be added, the sum will be 15?

2. What number is that, to which if its $\frac{1}{2}$ be added, the sum will be 24?

3. What number is that, to which if its $\frac{1}{3}$ be added, the sum will be 40?

4. What number is that, to which if its $\frac{1}{4}$ be added, the sum will be 30?

5. What number is that, to which if its $\frac{3}{5}$ be added, the sum will be 88?

6. How old is that man, to whose age if you add ⅛ and its ⅖, the sum will be 104 years?

7. What number is that, which being increased by its ½, its ⅓, and 18 more, will be doubled?

8. A man, being asked his age, said, my age increased by its ¾ and 20 more, is double my age. What was his age?

9. Suppose I buy a certain number of boxes of butter, at $2 a box, and as many more at $4 a box, and sell them all at $3 a box; do I gain or lose, and how much?

10. A boy, being asked how many oranges he had, replied, if my number were increased by its ⅔, its ¾, and 42 more, the sum would equal 3 times my number. How many had he?

11. Suppose I buy a certain number of melons; some at 10 cents each, and as many more at 40 cents each; and sell them all, at 30 cents apiece; how much do I gain on each melon?

12. If by selling 1 apple I lose $\frac{3}{20}$ of a cent, how many apples, at this rate, must I sell to lose 6 cents?

13. A boy bought a certain number of lemons, at 2 cents apiece, and as many more, at 4 cents apiece: and sold them at the rate of 3 for 5 cents: did he gain or lose, and how much?

14. A woman bought a certain number of apples, at the rate of 2 for a cent, as many more at the rate of 3 for a cent; and sold them all at the rate of 5 for 2 cents, and by so doing lost 4 cents. How many of each kind did she buy?

15. A woman bought a certain number of eggs, at the rate of 3 for a cent, and as many more, at 4 for a cent; and sold them out at the rate of 8 for 3 cents, and by so doing gained 4 cents. How many eggs did she buy?

16. Three men agreed to share $510 in the proportion of ½, ⅔, and ¼; how much must each receive?

17. A's fortune is to B's as $\frac{1}{2}$ is to $\frac{1}{3}$; and they together have $100; how much has each?

18. The difference of 2 numbers is 15, which is $\frac{3}{4}$ of twice as much as the smaller number; what are these two numbers?

19. A merchant bought a certain number of yards of cloth, at the rate of 2 yards for $1, and as many more, at the rate of 5 for $1; and sold them all at the rate of 10 yards for $3 ; and thereby lost $8. How many yards did he buy?

20. A man bought a certain number of melons, at the rate of 4 for $1, and as many more at the rate of 10 for $1 , and sold them all at the rate of 8 for $2, and thereby gained $6. How many melons did he buy?

Lesson XII.

1. Mary has twice as many apples as Sarah, and they together have 12; how many has each?

REMARK.—By the condition of the question Mary has 2 apples as often as Sarah 1. Consequently Mary must have $\frac{2}{3}$, and Sarah $\frac{1}{3}$ of the 12 apples.

2. Divide 18 into 2 such parts that one shall be twice the other?

3. Divide 21 oranges between two boys so that one may have twice as many as the other.

4. Franklin and Francis together have 15 quarts of nuts, but Franklin has twice as many as Francis ; how many has each?

5. Robert has twice as many cents as Harry, and together they have 24; how many has each?

6. Divide the number 27 into two parts, that shall be to each other as 1 to 2.

7. Harriet is twice as old as Ellen, and the sum of their ages is 30 years; what is the age of each?

8. A and B are 36 rods apart, and travel towards

each other; how far will each travel before they meet, provided A travel twice as fast as B?

9. What number must be added to twice itself, that the sum will be 57?

10. A, after spending $\frac{1}{4}$ of all his money and $\frac{2}{5}$ of the remainder less $4, had only $14 remaining; how much had he at first?

11. Divide the number 48 into two such parts, that one shall be $\frac{3}{5}$ of the other.

12. In a certain school, there are 8 times as many boys as girls, and in all there are 52 pupils; how many boys and how many girls in the school?

13. James and Jackson together have 45 marbles, but James has only $\frac{1}{4}$ as many as Jackson; how many has each?

14. A man and his son together earned $280 in a year; how much does each earn, provided the boy earns only $\frac{1}{3}$ as much as his father?

15. A boy bought a melon and a citron for $1; how much did each cost, provided the melon cost only $\frac{1}{3}$ as much as the citron?

16. A man bought a horse and a saddle for $120; the saddle cost only $\frac{1}{9}$ as much as the horse; what was the cost of each?

17. A man, being asked the cost of his oxen, said, my oxen and wagon together cost $240, and the oxen cost twice as much as the wagon; what was the cost of each?

18. A man bought a sheep, a hog, and a cow for $42; for the hog he gave twice as much as for the sheep, and for the cow, 3 times as much as for the sheep. How much did he give for each?

19. A farmer and his two sons earned $560 in 1 year; the father earned twice as much as his elder son, and the elder son earned twice as much as the younger son. How much did each earn?

20. A, B, and C together, in 1 day, can dig 105

bushels of potatoes; A digs $\frac{1}{2}$ as much as B, and B $\frac{1}{2}$ as much as C. How many bushels can each dig in a day?

21. A man bought three pieces of cloth for $160; the first piece only cost $\frac{1}{3}$ as much as the second, and the second only $\frac{1}{4}$ as much as the third. How much did each piece cost?

22. In an army consisting of 20,000 men, 3 times as many were wounded as were killed, and 4 times as many remained unhurt as were wounded. How many were killed, wounded and unhurt respectively?

23. $\frac{1}{2}$ of A's + $\frac{2}{3}$ of B's money equals $5500; and $\frac{2}{3}$ of B's money is 4 times $\frac{1}{2}$ of A's. How much money has each?

24. Herman and Byron together have 60 blocks; and Byron owns $\frac{2}{3}$ as many as Herman; how many has each?

25. Divide the number 60 into 2 parts, that shall be to each other as $\frac{1}{2}$ to $\frac{3}{4}$?

26. Adelia and Louisa are to share 14 apples in the proportion of 4 to 3; how many ought each to receive?

27. The sum of Mary and Hezekiah's age is 25 years; how old is each, provided Hezekiah is only $\frac{2}{3}$ as old as Mary?

28. Henry and his father can thrash 35 bushels of oats in a day; how many does each thrash, if Henry thrashes only $\frac{2}{3}$ as much as his father?

29. A pole, whose length is 70 feet, is in the air and water; how much is in the air and water respectively, if $\frac{3}{4}$ of the length in the air equals the length in the water?

30. Divide the number 36 into two parts that shall be to each other as 5 to 4

31. Divide the number 45 into 2 parts that shall be to each other as 1 to $\frac{1}{4}$.

32. A and B together own $480; but A owns only $\frac{2}{3}$ as much as B; how much belongs to each?

33. A man died, and left $7200 to be divided between his son and daughter, in the proportion of 1 to $\frac{2}{7}$. How much ought each to receive?

34. In a mixture of tea consisting of 48 pounds, there was $\frac{1}{3}$ as much poor as good tea; how much of each kind was there?

35. A man bought a cow and a horse for $96; the cow cost $\frac{3}{5}$ as much as the horse; how much was the cost of each?

36. Moses has only $\frac{3}{7}$ as many chestnuts as Aaron; and both have 40 quarts; how many belong to each?

37. Divide the number 49 into two parts, that shall be to each other as 1 to $\frac{2}{5}$.

38. A hound ran 60 rods before he caught a fox; and $\frac{2}{3}$ the distance the fox ran before he was caught equalled the distance he was ahead when they started. How far did the fox run, and how far in advance of the hound was he when the chase commenced?

39. The sum of two numbers is 140, and the larger is to the smaller as 1 to $\frac{5}{9}$; what are the two numbers?

40. A and B together owe $69, but B owes only $1\frac{1}{2}$ as much as A; how much does each owe?

41. Thomas and Thornton found $240, but could not agree about the division of it; they therefore threw it on the floor, and each got what he could; it so happened that Thomas got only $\frac{3}{5}$ as much as Thornton. How much did each get?

42. In a certain school, consisting of 48 pupils, there are $1\frac{2}{7}$ times as many boys as girls; how many boys and how many girls in the school?

43. A gold and a silver watch were bought for $160; the silver watch cost only $\frac{1}{7}$ as much as the gold one: how much was the cost of each?

44. Divide the number 17 into two parts, that shall be to each other as $\frac{2}{3}$ to $\frac{3}{4}$.

45. A farmer had 180 sheep in two fields, and $\frac{1}{4}$ of the number in the first field equalled $\frac{1}{5}$ of the number in the second; how many in each field?

46. Divide 88 into two parts that shall be to each other as $\frac{2}{3}$ to $\frac{4}{5}$.

47. $\frac{3}{5}$ of the distance a hare ran after a hound started in pursuit, equalled the distance she was before the hound when they started; how far did the hare run before she was caught, provided the hound ran 80 rods to overtake her?

48. A and B started from the same point, and ran in the same direction; B ran 60 rods; then $\frac{1}{11}$ of the distance A had run equalled the distance A was ahead of B. How much did A gain on B in running 60 rods?

49. A fishing-rod, the length of which is 24 feet, is in two parts; $\frac{2}{5}$ of the longer part equals the length of the shorter. How long is each part?

50. A hound ran 90 rods before he caught a deer; the deer ran 44 times as far as it was ahead of the hound when they started, before it was overtaken. How far ahead of the hound was the deer when the chase commenced?

51. $\frac{2}{3}$ of A's number of sheep + $\frac{3}{4}$ of B's number, equals 900; how many sheep has each, provided $\frac{3}{4}$ of B's number is twice $\frac{2}{8}$ of A's number?

Lesson XIII.

ı. A person had two silver cups, and only one cover for both. The first cup weighed 6 oz. If the first cup be covered, it will weigh twice as much as the second, but if the second cup be covered it will weigu 3 times as much as the first. What is the weight of the second cup and cover?

SOLUTION.—By the last condition of the question, 3 times 6 oz., the weight of the first cup, or 18 ounces, equals the weight of the second cup and cover. Consequently the two cups and cover weigh 18 + 6 ounces, which are 24 ounces. And by the first condition, the first cup and cover weigh twice as much as the second cup. Therefore the 24 ounces must be divided into two parts, which are to each other as 2 to 1. One of these parts will be the weight of the second cup, and 2 the weight of the first cup and cover, &c.

2 A lady has two silver cups, and only one cover for both. The first cup weighs 8 ounces. The first cup and cover weigh 3 times as much as the second cup; and the second cup and cover 4 times as much as the first cup. What is the weight of the second cup and cover?

3. A man bought a hat, a coat, and a vest for $40. The hat cost $6; the hat and coat cost 9 times as much as the vest. What was the cost of each?

4. A boy bought a squirrel, a rabbit, and a bird. The squirrel cost 15 cents. The squirrel and rabbit cost twice as much as the bird; and the rabbit and bird cost 3 times as much as the squirrel. What was the cost of the bird and rabbit respectively?

5. A farmer bought a cow, an ox, and a horse. The cow cost $20; the cow and ox together cost 3 times as much as the horse; the ox and horse together cost 4 times as much as the cow. What was the cost of the ox and horse respectively?

6. A man bought two horses and a saddle. The younger horse cost $40 ; the saddle cost—$\frac{1}{2}$ as much as both horses; and the younger horse cost $\frac{1}{3}$ as much as the other horse and saddle together. What did the saddle and older horse cost respectively?

7 A man travelled three successive days. The first day he travelled 30 miles, which was $\frac{1}{4}$ of the distance he travelled the other two days; and 4 times

the distance he travelled the second day equalled the distance he travelled the first and third days. How far did he travel each day?

8. A is worth $1000, and B and C together are worth 9 times as much as A; and C is worth $\frac{1}{8}$ as much as A and B.   How much is B and C worth respectively?

9. A's coat cost $20, and his vest and hat together cost 5 times as much as his coat; and 3 times the cost of his vest equalled the cost of both coat and hat. What was the cost of his vest and hat respectively?

10. B's harness cost $120, which was $\frac{1}{3}$ of the cost of his horse and sleigh; and the harness and horse together cost twice as much as the sleigh. How much did the horse and sleigh cost respectively?

11. A tree in falling broke into three unequal pieces.   The top piece was 8 feet long, which was $\frac{1}{6}$ of the length of the other two pieces; and 3 times the length of the bottom piece equals the length of the other two pieces.   How long was the tree, and how long was each piece?

12. Find the ages of A, B, and C, by knowing that A is 20 years old, and that the sum of B and C's age is 4 times A's age, and that C's age is $\frac{1}{8}$ of the sum of A and B's age.

13. Find the fortunes of A, B, C, D, E, and F, by knowing that A is worth $20, which is $\frac{1}{4}$ as much as B and C are worth, and that C is worth $\frac{1}{3}$ as much as A and B ; and, also, that if 19 times the sum of A, B, and C's fortune were divided in the proportion of $\frac{3}{4}$, $\frac{1}{2}$, and $\frac{1}{3}$, it would respectively give $\frac{3}{4}$ of D's, $\frac{1}{2}$ of E's, and $\frac{1}{3}$ of F's fortune.

14. A and B dug 100 rods of ditch for $100.   A received 10 shillings a rod and B 6 shillings a rod. How many rods did each dig, provided each received $50?   Ans. A dug $37\frac{1}{2}$ rods, and B $62\frac{1}{2}$.

NOTE.—Consider the above a Penn. or N. J. question.

CHAPTER VIII.

Lesson I.

REMARK.—In our calculations on interest, we shall reckon 30 days to the month, and 12 months to the year. Although this, mathematically speaking, will not produce a result *strictly accurate*, yet it will be sufficiently *correct* for all practical purposes.

1. Reduce 2 years and 4 months to the fraction of a year.

SOLUTION.—4 months is what part of a year? There are 12 months in 1 year, therefore 1 month is $\frac{1}{12}$ of a year; and 4 months are 4 times $\frac{1}{12}$, which are $\frac{4}{12}$ or $\frac{1}{3}$ of a year. In 2⅓ years how many thirds? In one there are $\frac{3}{3}$, therefore 3 times the number of whole ones equal the number of thirds. 3 times 2 are 6, and ⅓ are $\frac{7}{3}$ years.

☞ REMARK—*Always reduce a fraction to the lowest terms before performing any other operation with it.*☜

Pupils may not be able, readily, to discover the greatest number that will divide both *numerator* and *denominator*, without a remainder. Consequently, the most expeditious way will be, to continue to divide by the least number that is contained in both numerator and denominator without a remainder, until the fraction is reduced to its lowest terms.

2. Reduce 1 year and 3 months to the fraction of a year.

3. Reduce 3 years and 5 months to the fraction of a year.

4. Reduce 4 years and 10 months to the fraction of a year.

5. Reduce 7 years and 9 months to the fraction of a year.

6. Reduce 8 years and 8 months to the fraction of a year.

7. Reduce 12 years and 7 months to the fraction of a year.

8. Reduce 11 years and 11 months to the fraction of a year.

9. Reduce 6 years and 6 months to the fraction of a year.

10. Reduce 9 years and 8 months to the fraction of a year.

11. Reduce 2 years 4 months and 15 days to the fraction of a year.

SOLUTION.—15 days is what part of a month? There are 30 days in one month, therefore 1 day is $\frac{1}{30}$ of a month, and 15 days are 15 times $\frac{1}{30}$, which are $\frac{15}{30}$, or $\frac{1}{2}$ of a month. $4\frac{1}{2}$ months or $\frac{9}{2}$ months, is what part of a year? There are 12 months in 1 year, therefore 1 month is $\frac{1}{12}$ of a year, and $\frac{1}{2}$ of a month is $\frac{1}{2}$ of $\frac{1}{12}$; which is $\frac{1}{24}$ of a year; and if $\frac{1}{2}$ of a month is $\frac{1}{24}$ of a year, 9 halves are 9 times $\frac{1}{24}$, which are $\frac{9}{24}$, or $\frac{3}{8}$ of a year. $2\frac{3}{8}$ years equal $\frac{19}{8}$ years.

12. Reduce 4 years 7 months and 6 days to the fraction of a year.

13. Reduce 5 years 9 months and 18 days to the fraction of a year.

14. Reduce 1 year 7 months and 18 days to the fraction of a year.

15. Reduce 2 years 7 months and 6 days to the fraction of a year.

REMARK.—Omitting the intermediate steps in the analysis we have:

SOLUTION.—6 days is $\frac{6}{30}$, or $\frac{1}{5}$ of a month. $7\frac{1}{5}$ months equal $\frac{36}{5}$ months. $\frac{36}{5}$ months equal $\frac{3}{5}$ of a year. $2\frac{3}{5}$ years equal $\frac{13}{5}$ years.

16. Reduce 3 years 3 months and 6 days to the fraction of a year.

17. Reduce 5 years 4 months and 24 days to the fraction of a year.

18. Reduce 6 years 5 months and 18 days to the fraction of a year.

19. Reduce 7 years 11 months and 6 days to the fraction of a year.

20. Reduce 10 years 10 months and 12 days to the fraction of a year.

Lesson II.

REMARK.—*Interest* is money due for the use of money borrowed ; and is estimated at a certain rate per cent. per annum, which is regulated by law.

The sum on which the interest is paid is called the *Principal.* The sum of the *principal* and *interest* is called the *Amount.*

By 6 per cent. is meant, 6 cents on 100 cents, $6 on $100, or 6 on 100 whatever be the denomination. Hence, at 6 per cent. $\frac{6}{100}$ or $\frac{3}{50}$ of the principal equals the interest.

When no time is specified 1 year is understood.

1. At 4 per cent., what part of the principal equals the interest.

SOLUTION.—If the interest on 100 cents is 4 cents, of 1 cent it is $\frac{1}{100}$ of 4 cents, which is $\frac{4}{100}$ or $\frac{1}{25}$ of a cent. Therefore, at 4 per cent., $\frac{1}{25}$ of the principal equals the interest.

2. At 2 per cent., what part of the principal equals the interest?

3. At 5 per cent., what part of the principal equals the interest?

4. At 6 per cent., what part of the principal equals the interest?

5. At 8 per cent., what part of the principal equals the interest?

6. At 10 per cent., what part of the cost equals the gain?

7. At 7 per cent., what part of the principal equals the interest?

8. At 12 per cent., what part of the cost equals the gain?

9. At 18 per cent. what part of the cost equals the gain?

10. What is the interest of $80 for 1 year, at 15 per cent?

SOLUTION.—At 15 per cent., $\frac{15}{100}$, or $\frac{3}{20}$ of the principal equals the interest. $\frac{3}{20}$ of $80 is $12, the interest.

11. What is the interest of $120 for 1 year, at 25 per cent.?

12. What is the interest of $510 for 1 year, at 20 per cent.?

13. What is the interest of $750 for 1 year, at 24 per cent.?

14. A man paid $120 for a wagon, and sold it, at a gain of 30 per cent.; how much was his gain?

SOLUTION.—If he gained 30 per cent. he gained $\frac{30}{100}$, or $\frac{3}{10}$ of the cost. $\frac{3}{10}$ of $120 is $36, the gain.

15. A tailor sold a coat that cost him $25 at a gain of 32 per cent.; how much did he gain?

16. A man sold a quantity of goods that cost him $840, at a gain of 75 per cent.; how much did he gain?

17. Edward spent 85 per cent. of $120 for a suit of clothes; how much did his clothes cost him?

18. Henry's watch cost $180, he sold it at a loss of 15 per cent.; how much did he receive for it?

19. A boy sold a quantity of candies that cost him 50 cents, at a gain of 120 per cent.; how much did he receive for them?

20. Jacob sold a horse that cost him $240, at a loss of 25 per cent. how much did he receive for the horse?

Lesson III.

REMARK.—The principal or cost is always 100 per cent.

1. If $\frac{3}{50}$ of the principal equals the interest, what is the rate per cent.?

SOLUTION 1ST.—If $\frac{3}{50}$ of the principal equals the interest, the rate per cent. is $\frac{3}{50}$ of 100 per cent., which is 6 per cent.

SOLUTION 2ND.—If the interest of 1 cent is $\frac{3}{50}$ of a cent, the interest of 100 cents is 100 times $\frac{3}{50}$, or $\frac{300}{50}$, or 6 cents. Therefore it is 6 per cent.

2. If $\frac{1}{50}$ of the principal equals the interest, what is the rate per cent.?

3. If $\frac{2}{25}$ of the principal equals the interest, what is the rate per cent.?

4. If $\frac{9}{50}$ of the cost equals the gain, what is the rate per cent.?

5. If $\frac{3}{25}$ of the cost equals the gain, what is the rate per cent.?

6. If $\frac{1}{25}$ of the principal equals the interest, what is the rate per cent.?

7. If $\frac{1}{15}$ of the cost equals the gain, what is the rate per cent.?

8. If the interest of $44 for 1 year is $4, what is the rate per cent.?

SOLUTION.—If the interest of $44 is $4, $\frac{4}{44}$, or $\frac{1}{11}$ of the principal equals the interest. Therefore, the rate per cent. is $\frac{1}{11}$ of 100 per cent., which is 9 $\frac{1}{11}$ per cent.

9. If the interest of $72 for 1 year is $6, what is the rate per cent.?

10. If the interest of $96 for 1 year is $12, what is the rate per cent.?

11. B bought a horse for $100 and sold it for $109; how much did he gain per cent.?

12. A woman bought a quantity of oranges for 75 cents and sold them for 34 cents; how much did she gain per cent.?

13. A merchant bought a quantity of books for $200, and sold them for $228; how much did he gain per cent.?

14. If by laying out $37 I gain a sum equal to $\frac{2}{5}$ of it, what do I gain per cent.?

15. Harvey bought a hogshead of molasses for $25 and sold it for $31½; how much did he gain per cent.?

16. Bought a knife for 37 cents and sold it for 57½ cents; what was the gain per cent.?

17. A stationer sold a quantity of paper for $\frac{5}{4}$ of what it cost him; how much did he gain per cent.?

18. James received for his horse $\frac{7}{5}$ of what it co him; how much did he gain per cent.?

10

19. A man sold a barrel of pork for $\frac{7}{5}\frac{1}{0}$ of what it cost him; how much did he gain per cent.?

20. The interest of $500 for 4 years is $240; what is the rate per cent.?

SOLUTION.—If the interest of $500 for 4 years is $240, for 1 year it is $\frac{1}{4}$ of $240, or $60. Therefore, $\frac{60}{500}$, or $\frac{3}{25}$ of the principal equals the interest. If the interest of $1 for 1 year is $\frac{3}{25}$, the interest of $100 is 100 times $\frac{3}{25}$, or $\frac{300}{25}$, or $12. Therefore, it is 12 per cent.

21. A man, being asked, at what per cent. his money was on interest, replied, I receive $120 interest in 10 years for $240; what was his rate per cent.?

22. A bought a horse for $150 and sold it for $100; what was his gain per cent.?

23. Elisha bought 10 horses for $800, and sold 8 of them for what they all cost; what was his gain per cent.?

24. $\frac{7}{50}$ of the money C paid for books, is $\frac{1}{5}$ of what he gained by selling them. How much did he gain per cent.?

25. $\frac{3}{25}$ of the money I have on interest, is 4 times the yearly interest received. What is the rate per cent.?

26. $1\frac{3}{45}$ of the cost of A's merchandise, is $\frac{4}{3}$ of what he gained when he sold it. What was his gain per cent.?

27. $\frac{4}{75}$ of the cost of B's wagon, is $\frac{2}{3}$ of what he gained by selling it. What did he gain per cent.?

28. A book was sold for $\frac{2}{3}$ of $\frac{6}{5}$ of what it cost. What was the loss per cent.?

29. $\frac{3}{4}$ of $\frac{8}{5}$ of the cost of a sleigh, was what it was sold for. What was the gain per cent.?

30. A merchant bought a quantity of goods for $860 and sold them for $1075; how much did he gain per cent.?

Lesson IV.

1. At 5 per cent. for 4 years, what part of the principal equals the interest?

SOLUTION.—If the interest of $1 for 1 year is 5 cents, for 4 years it is 4 times 5 cents, or 20 cents. Therefore, $\frac{20}{100}$ or $\frac{1}{5}$ of the principal equals the interest.

2. At 6 per cent. for 5 years, what part of the principal equals the interest?

3. At 3 per cent. for 2 years, what part of the principal equals the interest?

4. At 4 per cent. for 3 years, what part of the principal equals the interest?

5. At 6 per cent. for 3 years, what part of the principal equals the interest?

6. At 4 per cent. for 3 years, what part of the principal equals the interest?

7. At 9 per cent. for 6 years, what part of the principal equals the interest?

8. At 8 per cent. for 5 years, what part of the principal equals the interest?

9. At 4 per cent. for 6 years, what part of the principal equals the interest?

10. At 6 per cent. for 5 years, what part of the principal equals the interest?

11. At 10 per cent. for 5 years, what part of the principal equals the interest?

12. At 6 per cent. for 4 years and 8 months, what part of the principal equals the interest?

REMARK.—It is expected that pupils thoroughly understand every lesson they have been over; and are, therefore, prepared to arrive at results, understandingly, without giving the entire analysis of all parts of the question.

SOLUTION.—8 months is $\frac{8}{12}$, or $\frac{2}{3}$ of a year. $4\frac{2}{3}$ years equal $\frac{14}{3}$ years. If the interest of $1 for 1 year is 6 cents, for $\frac{14}{3}$ years it is $\frac{14}{3}$ times 6 cents, or 28 cents. Therefore, $\frac{28}{100}$ or $\frac{7}{25}$ of the principal equals the interest.

13. At 4 per cent. for 6 years and 6 months, what part of the principal equals the interest?

14. At 6 per cent. for 5 years and 4 months, what part of the principal equals the interest?

15. At $10\frac{1}{2}$ per cent. for 1 year and 6 months, what part of the principal equals the interest?

16. At $4\frac{2}{3}$ per cent. for 9 years, what part of the principal equals the interest?

17. At $3\frac{3}{5}$ per cent. for 2 years and 2 months, what part of the principal equals the interest?

18. At $6\frac{1}{4}$ per cent. for 4 months and 24 days, what part of the principal equals the interest?

19. At $7\frac{1}{5}$ per cent. for 10 months, what part of the principal equals the interest?

20. At $3\frac{7}{19}$ per cent. for 2 years, 4 months and 15 days, what part of the principal equals the interest?

Lesson V.

1. What is the interest of $50 for 4 years, at 6 p.c

SOLUTION 1ST.—The interest of $1 for 4 years, at 6 per cent., is 24 cents; and for $50 it is 50 times 24 cents, or $12.

SOLUTION 2ND.—The interest of $1 for 4 years, at 6 per cent., is 24 cents. Therefore, $\frac{24}{100}$, or $\frac{6}{25}$ of the principal equals the interest. $\frac{6}{25}$ of $50 is $12, the interest.

2. What is the interest of $10 for 2 years, at 5 p.c.?

3. What is the interest of $48 for 6 years, at 5 p.c.?

4. What is the interest of $70 for 7 years, at 5 p.c.?

5. What is the interest of $68 for 5 years, at 6 p.c.?

6. What is the interest of $70 for 2 years, at 5 p.c.?

7. What is the interest of $75 for 5 years, at 3 p.c.?

8. What is the interest of $120 for 8 years, at 5 per cent.?

9. What is the interest of $100 for 10 years, at 6 per cent.?

10. What is the interest of $140 for 12 years, at 5 per cent?

11. What is the interest of $150 for 5 years, at 3 per cent.?

12. What is the interest of $145 for 6 years, at 5 per cent.?

13. What is the interest of $200 for 10 years, at 8 per cent.?

14. What is the interest of $250 for 3 years, at 8 per cent.?

15. What is the interest of $220 for 11 years, at 10 per cent.?

16. What is the interest of $500 for 9 years, at 8 per cent.?

17. What is the interest of $250 for 12 years, at 6 per cent.?

18. What is the interest of $500 for 8 years, at 12 per cent.?

19. What is the interest of $200 for 9 years, at 3 per cent.?

20. What is the interest of $405 for 10 years, at 8 per cent.?

21. What is the interest of $50 for 2 years and 2 months, at 6 per cent.?

SOLUTION.—2 months is $\frac{1}{6}$ of a year. $2\frac{1}{6}$ years equals $\frac{13}{6}$ years. If the interest of $1 for 1 year is 6 cents, for $\frac{13}{6}$ years it is $\frac{13}{6}$ times 6 cents, or 13 cents. Therefore, $\frac{13}{100}$ of the principal equals the interest. $\frac{13}{100}$ of $50 is $\frac{13}{2}$ or $6.50, the interest.

22. What is the interest of $25 for 4 years and 3 months, at 4 per cent.?

23. What is the interest of $80 for 5 years and 5 months, at 6 per cent.?

24. What is the interest of $60 for 8 years and 6 months, at 6 per cent.?

25. What is the interest of $240 for 3 years and 9 months, at 6 per cent.?

26. What is the interest of $75 for 4 years and 8 months, at 9 per cent?

27. What is the interest of $50 for 2 years and 9 months, at 6 per cent.?

28. What is the interest of $80 for 12 years and 10 months, at 6 per cent.?

29. What is the interest of $69 for 8 years and 4 months, at 2 per cent.?

30. What is the interest of $60 for 4 years and 8 months, at 3 per cent.?

31. What is the interest of $600 for 2 years 4 months and 15 days, at 4 per cent.?

SOLUTION.—15 days is $\frac{1}{2}$ of a month. 4$\frac{1}{2}$ months equals $\frac{9}{2}$ months. $\frac{9}{2}$ months equals $\frac{9}{24}$, or $\frac{3}{8}$ of a year. 2$\frac{3}{8}$ years equal $\frac{19}{8}$ years. If the interest of $1 for 1 year is 4 cents, for $\frac{19}{8}$ years it is $\frac{19}{8}$ times 4 cents, or $\frac{19}{2}$ cents. Therefore, $\frac{19}{200}$ of the principal equals the interest. $\frac{19}{200}$ of $600 is $57, the interest.

32. What is the interest of $300 for 5 years 9 months and 18 days, at 5 per cent.?

33. What is the interest of $550 for 4 years 7 months and 6 days, at 10 per cent.?

34. What is the interest of $500 for 1 year 7 months and 18 days, at 6 per cent.?

35. What is the interest of $250 for 3 years 7 months and 6 days, at 4 per cent.?

36. What is the interest of $250 for 3 years 3 months and 6 days, at 6 per cent.?

37. What is the interest of $50 for 6 years 4 months and 24 days, at 5 per cent.?

38. What is the interest of $75 for 2 years 11 months and 6 days, at 15 per cent.?

39. What is the interest of $150 for 2 years 10 months and 12 days, at 15 per cent.?

40. What is the interest of $300 for 2 years 9 months and 18 days, at 1 $\frac{4}{5}$ per cent. ?

Lesson VI.

1. What is the amount of $75 for 2 years, at 6 per cent. ?

SOLUTION.—If the interest of $1 for 1 year is 6 cents, for 2 years it is 2 times 6 cents, or 12 cents. Therefore $\frac{12}{100}$, or $\frac{3}{25}$, of the principal equals the interest. $\frac{3}{25}$ of $75 is $9, the interest; to which add $75, the principal, and we have $84, the amount.

2. What is the amount of $90 for 3 years, at 7 per cent. ?

3. What is the amount of $100 for 4 years, at 5 per cent. ?

4. What is the amount of $160 for 10 years, at 5 per cent. ?

5. What is the amount of $160 for 8 years, at 5 per cent. ?

6. What is the amount of $200 for 12 years, at 5 per cent?

7. What is the amount of $210 for 2 years and 6 months, at 4 per cent. ?

8. What is the amount of $250 for 4 years and 3 months, at 8 per cent. ?

9. What is the amount of $240 for 4 years and 2 months, at 3 per cent. ?

10. What is the amount of $500 for 3 years 3 months and 6 days, at 6 per cent. ?

11. What is the amount of $200 for 5 years 4 months and 24 days, at 5 per cent. ?

Lesson VII.

1. What principal will in 4 years, at 6 per cent., give $12 interest?

SOLUTION.—If the interest of $1 for 1 year is 6 cents, for 4 years it is 4 times 6 cents, or 24 cents. Therefore, $\frac{24}{100}$ or $\frac{6}{25}$ of the principal equals the interest, which is $12. If $\frac{6}{25}$ of the principal is $12, $\frac{1}{25}$ of the principal is $\frac{1}{6}$ of $12, or $2 ; and $\frac{6}{6}$ or the principal, is 25 times $2, or $50.

2. What principal will in 6 years, at 4 per cent., give $36 interest?

3. What principal will in 4 years, at 5 per cent., give $30 interest?

4. What principal will in 8 years, at 7 per cent., give $42 interest?

5. What principal will in 10 years, at 7 per cent., give $140 interest?

6. What principal will in 4 years and 6 months, at 6 per cent., give $54 interest?

7. What principal will in 4 years and 3 months, at 6 per cent., give $102 interest?

8. What principal will in 4 years and 3 months, at 8 per cent., give $51 interest?

9. How much money has that man on interest, who at the expiration of 4 years and 4 months, at 6 per cent., receives $260 interest?

10. At the expiration of 2 years and 4 months, at 6 per cent., a man received $49 interest; how much money had he on interest?

11. A is worth twice as much as B, and the interest of their united fortunes for 4 years and 2 months, at 6 per cent., is $600; how much is each worth?

12. The interest on the cost of B's store and house, for 1 year and 6 months, at 4 per cent., would be $270. What was the cost of each, provided the store cost $\frac{1}{4}$ as much as the house?

13. If the money B paid for a sheep, a cow, and horse, was put on interest for 4 years and 6 months, at 4 per cent., it would give $18 interest. What was the cost of all, and of each respectively, provided the sheep cost $\frac{1}{3}$ as much as the cow, and the cow $\frac{1}{4}$ as much as the horse?

Lesson VIII.

1. What principal will in 4 years, at 5 per cent., amount to $360?

SOLUTION.—If the interest of $1 for 1 year is 5 cents, for 4 years it is 4 times 5 cents, or 20 cents. Therefore, $\frac{20}{100}$, or $\frac{1}{5}$ of the principal, equals the interest: to which add $\frac{5}{5}$, the principal, and we have $\frac{6}{5}$ of the principal, equal to the amount $360. If $\frac{6}{5}$ of the principal is $360, $\frac{1}{5}$ of the principal is $\frac{1}{6}$ of $360, which is $60, and $\frac{5}{5}$ (the principal) is 5 times $60, which are $300.

2 What principal will in 3 years, at 6 per cent., amount to $118?

3. What principal will in 6 years, at 10 per cent., amount to $120?

4. What principal will in 10 years, at 7 per cent., amount to $170?

5. What principal will in 4 years, at 5 per cent., amount to $660?

6. A is worth $\frac{1}{3}$ as much as B; and the interest on their united fortunes for 2 years, at 5 per cent., is $880. What is each of their fortunes?

7. A merchant sold a quantity of cloth for $214, and thereby gained 7 per cent. What did the cloth cost him?

8. What principal will in 2 years, at 7 per cent., amount to $1140?

9. What principal will in 10 years and 8 months, at 9 per cent., amount to $490?

10. The amount due on a note, which had been on interest 6 years and 2 months, at 6 per cent., was $274. What was the face of the note?

11. What principal will in 12 years and 9 months, at 4 per cent., amount to $302?

12. If $\frac{1}{2}$ of A's fortune for 4 years and 6 months. at 6 per cent., amounts to $127, what is his whole fortune?

13. If $\frac{2}{3}$ of B's fortune, being put on interest for

3 years 3 months and 6 days, at 15 per cent., amount to $149, what is his whole fortune?

14. Mary, being asked how much money she had on interest, and at what per cent., replied: the principal and rate per cent. are such that in 5 years the amount would be $750, and in 7 years, $810; what was the principal and the rate per cent.?

15. A man sold two horses for $240, losing on the first 20 per cent., gaining on the other 20 per cent.; what was the value of each horse, provided he received for the second 3 times as much as for the first?

16. The amount of Robert's capital for a certain time, at 4 per cent., is $360, and for the same time, at 7 per cent., it is $405; required his capital and the time.

————

Lesson IX.

1. In what time will $40, at 6 per cent., give $12 interest?

SOLUTION.—If the interest of $40 is $12, $\frac{12}{40}$, or $\frac{3}{10}$ of the principal equals the interest. If the interest of $1 for 1 year is $\frac{3}{10}$ of a dollar, of $100 it is 100 times $\frac{3}{10}$, or $30. If it require 1 year for $100 to give $6 interest, to give $30 interest it will require as many years as $6 is contained times in $30, or 5 years.

2. In what time will $60, at 5 per cent., give $18 interest?

3. In what time will $90, at 7 per cent., give $27 interest?

4. In what time will $100, at 6 per cent., give $10 interest?

5. In what time will $120, at 10 per cent., give $120 interest?

6. In what time will $250, at 6 per cent. give $20 interest?

7. In what time will $40, at 7 per cent., give $8.40 interest?

8. In what time, at 8 per cent., will $30 give $9.60 interest?

9. In what time, at 6 per cent., will $10 give $2.40 interest?

10. In what time, at 4 per cent., will $20 give $5.60 interest?

Lesson X.

1 At what per cent. will $50, in 1 year and 6 months, or (1½ years), give $6 interest?

SOLUTION.—If the interest of $50 for 1½, or ¾ years is $6, for ½ of a year it is ⅓ of $6, or $2; and for ⅔, or 1 year, it is 2 times $2, or $4. Therefore, $\frac{4}{50}$, or $\frac{2}{25}$ of the principal equals the annual interest. If the interest of $1 for 1 year is $\frac{2}{25}$, of $100, it is 100 times $\frac{2}{25}$, or $8. Therefore, it is 8 per cent.

2. At what per cent. will $40 annually give $2 interest?

3. At what per cent. will $80 annually give $3.20 interest?

4. At what per cent. will $120 annually give $12 interest?

5. At what per cent. will $120, in 4 years, give $20 · interest?

6. At what per cent. will $100, in 3 years, give $30 interest?

7. At what per cent. will $5, in 14 years, give $7 interest?

8. At what per cent. will $25, in 1 year and 9 months, give $3.50 interest?

9. At what per cent. will $80, in 5 years and 8 months, give $34 interest?

10 At what per cent. will $500, in 7 years and 6 months, give $15 interest?

11. At what per cent. will $600, in 2 years 4 mon and 15 days, give $57 interest?

Lesson XI.

1. At what per cent., will $10 in 4 years, amount to $12?

REMARK.—From the amount subtract the principal, and the remainder will be interest. Then proceed as in the preceding lesson.

2. At what per cent. will $12, in 3 years, amount to $13.44?

3. At what per cent. will $20, in 6 years, amount to $26?

4. At what per cent. will $24, in 10 years, amount to $36?

5. At what per cent. will $30, in 7 years, amount to $36.30?

6. At what per.cent. will $50, in 10 years, amount to $75?

7. At what per cent. will $36, in 5 years, amount to $39.60?

8. At what per cent. will a given principal double itself in 20 years?

SOLUTION.—A given principal will double itself in 1 year, at 100 per cent. ; and in 20 years, at $\frac{1}{20}$ of 100 per cent., or 5 per cent.

9. At what per cent. will a given principal double itself in 4 years?

10. At what per cent. will a given principal double itself in 3 years?

11. At what per cent. will a given principal double itself in 5 years?

12. At what per cent. will $80 in 7 years give $80 interest?

13. At what per cent. will $640, in 6 years, give $640 interest?

14. At what per cent. will 25 cents, in 8 years, give 25 cents interest?

15. At what per cent. will $97, in 9 years, give $97 interest?

16. At what per cent. will $372, in 25 years, give $372 interest?

17. At what per cent. will $1, in 30 years, give $1 interest?

18. At what per cent. will $15, in $12\frac{1}{2}$ years, give $15 interest?

19. At what per cent. will $42, in $14\frac{1}{4}$ years, give $42 interest?

20. At what per cent. will 5 cents, in $16\frac{2}{3}$ years, give 5 cents interest?

Lesson XII.

1. In what time will a given principal double itself, at 5 per cent.?

SOLUTION.—A given principal will double itself in 100 years, at 1 per cent., and at 5 per cent., in $\frac{1}{5}$ of 100 years, which is 20 years.

2. In what time will a given principal double itself, at 4 per cent.?

3. In what time will $25, at 3 per cent. give $25 interest?

4. In what time will $275, at 6 per cent.. give $275 interest?

5. In what time will a given principal double itself, at 2 per cent.?

6. In what time will $4, at 7 per cent., give $4 interest?

7. In what time will $94, at 9 per cent., give $94 interest?

14

8. In what time will 5 cents, at 8 per cent. give 5 cents interest?

9. In what time will $3⅗, at 10 per cent., give $3⅗ interest?

10. In what time will 1 dime, at 12½ per cent., give 1 dime interest?

Lesson XIII.

1. Bought a bushel of grass-seed for $5, and sold it for $7; what was the gain per cent.?

SOLUTION.—Since it was bought for $5 and sold for $7, the gain must have been $7—$5, which is $2. Therefore, ⅖ of the cost equals the gain. If on $1 I gain $⅖, on $100 I will gain 100 times $⅖, or $40. Therefore, the gain is 40 per cent.

2. A book was bought for $2, and sold for $3; what was the gain per cent.?

3. A shawl cost $5, and was sold for $8; what was the gain per cent.?

4. A cow was bought for $20, and sold for $25; what was the gain per cent.?

5. A merchant bought a hogshead of molasses for $80, and sold it for $95; what did he gain per cent.?

6. A barrel of pork cost $12, and was sold for $11; what was the loss per cent.?

7. A horse was bought for $140, and sold for $60; what was the loss per cent.?

8. Bought an orange for 4 cents, and sold it for 6 cents; what was the gain per cent.?

9. Bought a melon for 15 cents, and sold it for 20 cents; what was the gain per cent.?

10. Bought a book for 5 dimes, and sold it for 8 dimes; what was the gain per cent.?

11. Bought a quantity of silk for $120, and sold it for $200; what was the gain per cent.?

12. A boy sold melons, at the rate of 10 cents

apiece, $\frac{1}{5}$ of which equaled his gain; how much would he have gained per cent., if he had sold them at 12 cents apiece?

13. A merchant sold sugar, for $80 a hogshead, and thereby cleared $\frac{1}{10}$ of his money; if he had sold it at $92 a hogshead, what would he have gained per cent.?

14. A quantity of cloth was bought for $36, and sold for $43; what was the gain per cent.?

15. A horse was bought for $100, and sold for $95; what was the loss per cent.?

16. A man sold a horse for $120, and thereby cleared $\frac{1}{5}$ of its cost; how much would he have lost per cent. if he had sold him for $80?

17. What per cent. of $\frac{1}{3}$ is $\frac{1}{6}$? Of $\frac{2}{3}$ is $\frac{1}{6}$? Of $\frac{2}{5}$ is $2\frac{1}{5}$? Of $\frac{3}{4}$ is $\frac{2}{3}$? Of $\frac{7}{8}$ is $\frac{2}{3}$? Of $2\frac{1}{2}$ is $\frac{2}{3}$? Of $3\frac{1}{5}$ is $2\frac{1}{10}$?

18. $\frac{2}{3}$ of $6 is what per cent. of $\frac{4}{5}$ of $100?

19. $\frac{5}{7}$ of $28 is $\frac{2}{3}$ of what per cent. of $\frac{5}{6}$ of $300?

20. Walter sold a horse for $120, and thereby cleared $\frac{1}{6}$ of its cost; what would he have lost per cent. by selling it for $80?

Lesson XIV

1. A man bought a cow for $20; for what must he sell her, to gain 5 per cent. on the cost?

SOLUTION.—If he gains 5 per cent. he gains $\frac{5}{100}$ or $\frac{1}{20}$ of the cost. $\frac{1}{20}$ of $20 is $1, the gain. Therefore, to gain 5 per cent. he must sell the cow for $20+$1, or $21.

2. A man bought a yoke of oxen for $100; how must he sell them, to gain 6 per cent. on the cost?

3. A man bought a barrel of rum for $10; for what must he sell it, to gain 10 per cent. on the cost?

4. A gallon of wine was bought for 20 dimes; how must it be sold a pint, to gain 20 per cent. on the cost?

5. A hogshead of molasses cost $20; for what ought it to be sold a gallon, to gain 40 per cent. on the cost?

6. B bought a horse for $80, and by selling it, lost 5 per cent. on the cost; for what did he sell it?

7. A wagon cost $140, and was sold for 5 per cent. less than it cost; for what was it sold?

8. A merchant, by selling 40 yards of cloth for $164, lost 20 per cent. on the cost; what did it cost per yard?

9. If a quart of brandy cost 50 cents, how must it be sold a gill, to lose 4 per cent.?

10. B lost 5 per cent. by selling a gallon of rum, which cost 80 cents · for what did he sell it a gallon?

Lesson XV.

1. What principal will, in 4 years, at 5 per cent., amount to $60?

SOLUTION.—If the interest of $1 for 1 year is 5 cents., for 4 years it is 4 times 5 cents., or 20 cents. Therefore, $\frac{20}{100}$, or $\frac{1}{5}$ of the principal, equals the interest; to which add $\frac{5}{5}$, the principal, and we have $\frac{6}{5}$ of the principal, equal to the amount, or $60. If $\frac{6}{5}$ of the principal is $60, $\frac{1}{5}$ of the principal is $\frac{1}{6}$ of $60, which is $10; and $\frac{5}{5}$, (the principal), is 5 times $10, which are $50.

2. What principal will, in 3 years, at 6 per cent. amount to $118?

3. What principal will, in 5 years, at 6 per cent., amount to $130?

4. What principal will, in 7 years, at 5 per cent., amount to $81?

5. What principal will, in 9 years, at 8 per cent., amount to $86?

6. What principal will, in $3\frac{3}{4}$ years, at 8 per cent., amount to $260?

7. What principal will, in $4\frac{2}{3}$ years, at 6 per cent., amount to $640?

8. What principal will, in $5\frac{5}{7}$ years, at 7 per cent., amount to $42?

9. What principal will, in $6\frac{3}{7}$ years, at 7 per cent., amount to $87?

10. What principal will, in $8\frac{2}{3}$ years, at 6 per cent., amount to $76?

REMARK.—The *present worth* of a debt payable at some future time, without interest, is such a sum as will, in the given time, and at the given rate per cent., amount to the debt. Hence the *present worth* of any sum of money, payable at some future time without interest, may be found in the same way that we found the *principal*, when we had given the amount, time, and rate per cent.

See the above solution.

11. What is the present worth of $26, due 5 years hence, at 6 per cent.? *Ans.* $20.

12. What is the present worth of $14, due 8 years ~ per cent.?

'he present worth of $110, due 5 years

21. What is the present worth of $186, due $4\frac{1}{5}$ years hence, at 5 per cent.?

22. What is the present worth of $66, due $5\frac{1}{3}$ years hence, at 6 per cent.?

23. What is the present worth of $128, due $4\frac{2}{3}$ years hence, at 6 per cent.?

Lesson XVI.

1. If I sell cloth at $2.50 a yard, and thereby gain 25 per cent., what did it cost a yard?

Solution.—If I gain 25 per cent. I gain $\frac{1}{4}$ of the cost; to which add $\frac{4}{4}$, the cost, and I have $\frac{5}{4}$ of the cost, equal to $2.50. If $\frac{5}{4}$ of what I gave for it is $2.50, $\frac{1}{4}$ of the cost is $\frac{1}{5}$ of $2.50, or 50 cents; and $\frac{4}{4}$ (the cost) is 4 times 50 cents, which are 200 cents, or $2.

2. A horse was sold for $38, which was at a loss of 5 per cent.; what did the horse cost?

3. If I sell cloth at $2.50 a yard, and thereby gain 25 per cent., how must I sell it a yard, to lose 20 per cent.?

4. If I sell cloth at $4.40 a yard, and thereby gain 10 per cent., how ought I to sell it, to lose 25 per cent.?

5. If by selling a piece of cloth for $46 I gain 15 per cent., how ought I to have sold it, to have lost 30 per cent.?

6. A sold his horse for $105, and thereby gained 5 per cent. on the cost; for what ought he to have sold it, to have lost 10 per cent.?

7. A farm was sold for $495, which was 10 per cent. less than what it was worth; for what ought it to have been sold, to have received 40 per cent. more than its value?

8. A mechanic lost 20 per cent. on the cost of a wagon, by selling it for $40; for what ought it to have been sold, to have gained 30 per cent.?

9. A horse was sold for $90, which was 10 per cent. less than its value; what would have been the gain per cent. if it had been sold for $120?

10. A farm was sold for $600, which was 8 per cent. less than its value; what would have been the gain per cent. if it had been sold for $850?

11. A book was sold for 90 cents, which was 10 per cent. less than its value; what would have been the gain per cent. if it had been sold for $1.50?

12. A man sold two watches, at $12 each; on one he gained 50 per cent., and on the other he lost 50 per cent. Did he gain or lose by the bargain, and how much?

13. An individual sold two gold pencils, at $6 apiece; on one he gained 20 per cent., and on the other he lost 20 per cent. Did he gain or lose, and how much?

14. A farmer sold two horses at $210 apiece; for one he received 25 per cent. more than its value, and for the other 25 per cent. less than its value. Did he gain or lose by the bargain, and how much?

15. A merchant sold a quantity of cloth for $280, and by so doing lost 60 per cent.; he then sold another quantity for $80, and thereby gained 60 per cent. Did he gain or lose by the operation, and how much?

Lesson XVII.

1. An individual was ordered to collect $190, and his own fee, which is to be 5 per cent. on all the money collected. How much should he receive?

SOLUTION.—He is to receive 5 per cent., or $\frac{1}{20}$ or $\frac{1}{20}$ of all he collects. $\frac{19}{20}$, all he collects, minus $\frac{1}{20}$, his fee, equals $\frac{19}{20}$ of all he collects, or $190, the amount he is to pay his employer. If $\frac{19}{20}$ of what he collects equals $190, $\frac{1}{20}$ if $\frac{1}{20}$ of $190, which is $10; and $\frac{2,8}{2,8}$ (what he collects) is 20 times $10, or $200. Therefore he must receive $200 — $190 = $10.

2. How much ought A to receive for collecting $90 and his own fee of 10 per cent. on all he collects?

3. What amount of money will be sufficient to pay a debt of $38 and the collectors' fee, which is 5 per cent. on all the money collected?

4. How much cider must that man make to bring away 15 barrels, after the owner of the mill receives $16\frac{2}{3}$ per cent. of all he has made?

5. How much grain must a farmer take to mill, that he may bring away the flour of 1 bushel, after the miller has taken 10 per cent. of all he took there?

Miscellaneous Questions.

1. At 5 per cent. for 4 years, what part of the principal equals the interest?

2. In how many years, at 4 per cent., will a given principal amount to the same as it would in 8 years, at 6 per cent?

3. At what per cent. will a given principal, in 14 years, amount to the same as it would in 12 years at 7 per cent.

4. If $\frac{1}{20}$ of the principal equals the interest, what is the rate per cent.?

5. The rent of B's farm, for 8 years, amounted to $\frac{3,2}{3,0}$ of its value. What per cent. did he annually receive on the value of his farm?

6. What is the interest of $75, for $5\frac{2}{3}$ years, at 6 per cent.?

7. What principal will, in $7\frac{1}{2}$ years, at 8 per cent., give $24 interest?

8. What principal, will in $4\frac{1}{5}$ years, at 5 per cent., amount to $155?

9. At what per cent. will a given principal double itself in $12\frac{1}{2}$ years?

10. The interest of A's and B's fortune, for 8 years, at 5 per cent., is $420. What is the fortune of each, provided A's fortune is twice B's?

11. The interest of $\frac{2}{3}$ of A's and $\frac{3}{4}$ of B's fortune, for 7 years at 5 per cent., is $2100. What is each of their fortunes, provided $\frac{2}{3}$ of A's fortune equals $\frac{3}{4}$ of B's?

12. B sold his horse for $\frac{1}{2}$ of $1\frac{1}{2}$ times what it cost; what did he lose per cent.?

13. What is the interest of $540 for 4 years at 5 per cent?

14. What is the interest of $180, for 5 years and 9 months, at $6\frac{2}{3}$ per cent?

15. What principal will, in 4 years 7 months and 6 days, at $6\frac{1}{4}$ per cent., amount to $412?

16. The interest of the cost of B's horse, sleigh, and wagon, for 6 years, at 5 per cent., is $69. What is the cost of each, provided their prices are to each other respectively, as $\frac{1}{2}$, $\frac{2}{3}$ and $\frac{3}{4}$?

17. What principal will, in 8 years and 8 months, at $7\frac{4}{5}$ per cent. amount to $419?

18. What principal will, in 5 years 9 months and 18 days, at 10 per cent., give $116 interest?

19. In what time will $420, at 5 per cent., give $147 interest?

20. If the interest of $200, for 1 year and 6 months, is $18, what is the rate per cent.?

21. At what per cent. will $500, in 4 years and 9 months, give $190 interest?

22. At what per cent. will $500, in 22 years and 6 days, amount to $1821?

23. At what per cent. will a given principal double itself in 20 years?

24. In what time will a given principal double itself at $12\frac{1}{2}$ per cent?

25. At what per cent. will a given principal double itself in 6 years and 8 months?

26. A horse was bought for $60, and sold for $90; what was the gain per cent.?

27. A basket containing 39 oranges cost $1.20; how must they be sold apiece to gain 30 per cent.?

28. If one quart of champagne cost 40 cents, how must it be sold a gill to gain 20 per cent.?

29. What is the present worth of $68, due 10 years hence, at 7 per cent.?

30. What is the discount on $162, due 10 years and 4 months hence, at 6 per cent.?

31. What is th present worth of $87, due $3\frac{1}{5}$ years hence, at 5 per cent.?

32. If a hogshead of molasses, containing 84 gallons, cost $30; how must it be sold a gallon, to gain 40 per cent.?

33. The money I have on interest, in 9 years, at 10 per cent. amounts to $190; what is the principal?

34. When money was worth 6 per cent. I bought $400 worth of goods; 6 months afterwards I sold them, and gained 10 per cent. on the cost. How much did I gain?   *Ans.* $28.

35. A speculator bought a horse for $36, and sold it for 25 per cent. more than he gave for it; which, however, was 10 per cent. less than what he asked for it. How much did he ask for the horse?

36. A gentleman being asked how much money he had on interest, replied, that if instead of 6 per cent. he should receive 10 per cent. he would receive $268 interest more than he did then. How much money had he on interest?

37. A merchant bought broadcloth for $1.20 a yard, and sold it for $33\frac{1}{3}$ per cent. more than he gave for it, which, however, was $33\frac{1}{3}$ per cent. less than his marked price for it. How much was his marked price per yard?

38. A merchant sold a quantity of cloth for $120, and by so doing gained 50 per cent. He then sold another quantity for $120, and thereby lost 50 per cent. Did he gain or lose by the bargain, and how much?

39. B sold a horse for $60, and gained 20 per cent. He then sold another horse for $60, and lost 60 per cent. Did he gain or lose, and how much?

40. The interest on $1\frac{1}{3}$ times A's, and $\frac{3}{5}$ of B's fortune, for 8 years, at 5 per cent., is $520. What is the fortune of each, provided $1\frac{1}{3}$ times A's fortune equals $\frac{2}{5}$ of B's?

41. $\frac{2}{3}$ of D's fortune added to $\frac{3}{4}$ of E's, which is 3 times $\frac{2}{3}$ of D's, being put on interest for 8 years, at 5 per cent., gives $800 interest. What is the fortune of each?

42. The interest of A's, B's, and C's fortune, for 5 years, at 8 per cent., is $1040. What is the fortune of each, provided they are to each other as $\frac{1}{2}$, $\frac{1}{3}$, and $\frac{1}{4}$?

43. The interest of A's, B's, and C's fortune, for $5\frac{1}{3}$ years, at 6 per cent. is $800. What is each of their fortunes, provided B's is twice A's, and B's and C's are equal?

44. A's fortune added to $\frac{2}{3}$ of B's, which is to A's as 2 to 3, being put on interest for 6 years, at 4 per cent., amounts to $124. What is the fortune of each?

45. D's money added to 4 times E's, which is equal to D's, being on interest for 10 years, at 5 per cent., amounts to $3000. What was each of their fortunes?

46. The sum of $\frac{2}{3}$ of A's $+ \frac{1}{2}$ of B's money, being on interest for 8 years, at 5 per cent., amounts to $2100. Provided $\frac{1}{2}$ of B's money is twice $\frac{2}{3}$ of A's, how much money has each?

47. $\frac{2}{5}$ of the cost of C's house, increased by $\frac{2}{5}$ of the cost of his farm, being placed on interest for 10 years, at 7 per cent., amounts to $17,000. What is the cost

of each, if $\frac{2}{5}$ of the cost of the house is only $\frac{1}{4}$ of $\frac{2}{3}$ of the cost of the farm?

48. If $\frac{5}{7}$ of A's fortune in 2 years and 4 months, at 6 per cent., amounts to $570, what is his whole fortune?

49. The sum of A's and B's fortune in 4 years and 8 months, at 6 per cent., amounts to $256. What was each of their fortunes, provided $\frac{2}{3}$ of A's fortune equals B's?

50. The interest for 5 years, at 6 per cent., on $\frac{2}{3}$ of the money Morgan owes, is $180; and the interest for the same time and rate per cent., on $\frac{2}{5}$ of the money due him is $120. How much has Morgan after paying his debts?

51. The money John paid for a sheep, a cow, and a horse, in 8 years, at ten per cent., would give such an interest, as would in $\frac{3}{4}$ as long, at $\frac{1}{4}$ as great a per cent., amount to $104; how much did he pay for each, provided the sheep cost $\frac{1}{2}$ as much as the cow, and the cow $\frac{1}{3}$ as much as the horse?

52. The interest of the sum of $\frac{1}{2}$ of Simpson's $\frac{2}{5}$ of Eyer's, and $\frac{5}{12}$ of Domer's fortune for 3 years 7 months and 6 days, at 10 per cent., is such as will in the same time, at $\frac{1}{2}$ the rate per cent., amount to $531. What is the fortune of each, provided $1\frac{1}{2}$ times Domer's part of the principal equals $\frac{3}{4}$ of Eyer's, and $\frac{7}{10}$ of Eyer's part of the principal equals $\frac{1}{5}$ of Simpson's?

53. The interest of the sum of $\frac{1}{2}$ of A's, and $\frac{2}{3}$ of B's fortune, for a *certain* time, at 2 per cent., was to *this sum* as 9 to 250. And the amount of *this interest* for 25 times as long, at 10 times as great a per cent., was $180. What was each of their fortunes, provided A's fortune was to B's as 1 to 3? And how long was the first on interest?

REMARK.—Since the interest was to the principal as 9 to 250, $\frac{9}{250}$ of the principal equals the interest. Hence 1 year 9 months and 18 days is the time required, &c.

QUESTIONS, QUERIES AND PUZZLES,

FOR

PUPILS AT HOME.

1. A hound is in pursuit of a fox that is 10 rods ahead of him, and *while* the hound runs 10 rods the fox runs 1 rod, (*i. e.* while the hound runs a certain distance, the fox runs one-tenth of that distance.) Will the hound overtake the fox? The conditions remaining the same, what is the greatest distance they can run?

2. A hound is in pursuit of a fox that is ten rods ahead of him, and *while* the fox runs 1 rod the hound runs 10 rods. How far will the hound run before he overtakes the fox?

3. Place four 5's in such a position that they shall equal 6¼.

4. A boy was sent to a spring with a 5 and a 3 quart measure to procure exactly 4 quarts of water. How did he measure it?

5. What is the difference between twice 25, and twice 5 and 20?

6. A man had 9 pigs and put them in 4 pens, with an odd number of pigs in each pen. How did he divide them?

7. Two men have an 8 gallon cask full of wine, which they desire to divide equally between them. How can they effect this division, provided the only measures they have are a 5 gallon cask and a 3 gallon cask?

8. Place four 2's in such a manner that they shall exactly equal 23.

9. Place 9 apples in 10 rows so that each row shall contain 3 apples.

10. A squirrel finding 9 ears of corn in a box, took from it daily, 3 *ears;* how many days was he in removing the corn from the box?

11. If from *six* you take IX, and from IX you take ten; and if fifty from forty be taken, there will then just half a dozen remain.

12. Edward, Maria, and their mother went to market. Edward had 60 apples and sold them, at 2 for 1 cent; Maria had 60 apples and sold them at 3 for 1 cent. Their mother had 120 apples and sold them at the rate of 5 for 2 cents. Which received the most, the children or the mother, and why?

13. A gentleman desiring to see an inmate of a prison, was asked by the keeper whether he was related to the culprit. He replied: "Brothers and sisters have I none, but his father is my father's son." What relation was the gentleman to the prisoner?

14. A man having a fox, a goose, and a peck of corn, was desirous of crossing a river. He could take only *one* across at a time, and if he left the fox and goose, while he took the corn over, the fox would kill the goose; but if he left the goose and corn, the goose would eat the corn. How shall he get them all safely across the river?

15. A snail wants to get up a wall 20 feet in height; during the day it climbs 5 feet, but slips back 4 feet every night. How many days would it take to reach the top?

16. A man purchased a hat for $5, and handed the merchant a $50 bill to pay for it. The merchant being unable to make the change, sent the bill to a broker, got it changed, and then gave the man who bought the hat $45. The broker, after the purchaser of the hat had gone, discovered that the bill was counterfeit, and therefore returned it to the merchant and received $50 good money. How much did the merchant lose by the operation?

17. Place ten pennies in a row, then carry one over two, leaving it upon the third, and continue doing this until the ten pennies occupy only five places with two in each place.

18. Two boys laid a wager as to which could lift the most. One lifted ninety-nine pounds, and the other a hundred, and *con.* How many pounds did both lift?

19. A frog at the bottom of a well, 10 feet deep, ascends 3 feet every jump. How many jumps must he take to get out?

20. A drover being asked how many horses he had, replied: "My horses together have twenty *fore*legs." How many horses had he?

21. Write 12 in such a manner, that you can show its half to be 7.

22.   "I am constrained to plant a grove
    To please the lady that I love.
    This ample grove is to compose
    Nineteen trees in nine straight rows·
    Five trees in each row I must place,
    Or I shall never see her face."

23. Do the waters of the Mississippi river flow up hill?

24. If a man should start from the city of New York, at 12 o'clock on Monday, and travel directly west for 24 hours, at the rate of 15 degrees an hour, it is evident he would then have reached New York again. It was Monday, 12 o'clock, when he started, and has been midday to him during his journey; (the sun being in his meridian); on his return to New York city it is Tuesday, 12 o'clock; at what point on his journey did it change from *Monday* to *Tuesday noon?*

25. Arrange in a square the numbers from 1 to 16, in such a manner that they shall amount to the same in each column, whether added perpendicularly, horizontally, diagonally, or taking any four of the numbers in the form of a square.

1	12	6	15
8	13	3	10
11	2	16	5
14	7	9	4

MAGIC SQUARES—AN EAST INDIA PUZZLE.

PUZZLE.—Take any odd number whatever—square it, and write the series of figures from one to the square of the number taken, in a square whose size is indicated by the number taken, in such a manner that the figures added horizontally, perpendicularly or diagonally, shall equal the same sum.

EXAMPLE.—Take the number 5,—its square is 25,—write the figures from 1 to 25 in a square made up of twenty-five smaller squares in such a manner that, added perpendicularly, horizontally, or diagonally, the sum shall be the same, that is, one-fifth of the sum of the series of numbers, 1 to 25,—and so of the numbers, 7, 9, 11, etc.

RULE.—Begin by placing 1 in the middle square at the top, then, in filling up, observe these directions according to the position of the square just filled, viz.: Proceed diagonally upward to the right, or if you cannot do this go to the square on the opposite side of the parallelogram in the next line at the right, or next line above; or if you can not do this, take the square immediately below.

These figures can be varied in at least *four* different ways. If the number 7 be taken, they can be varied *six* different ways; if 9 be taken, they can be varied *eight* different ways,—perhaps more.

17	24	1	8	15
23	5	7	14	16
4	6	13	20	22
10	12	19	21	3
11	18	25	2	9